The CANADIAN STORY

by MAY McNEER *with lithographs by*

LYND WARD · *Ariel Books* · *New York*

To our friends in Algoma

ARIEL BOOKS IS A DIVISION OF FARRAR, STRAUS AND CUDAHY, INC. COPYRIGHT © 1958 BY MAY
MCNEER WARD AND LYND WARD. LIBRARY OF CONGRESS CATALOG CARD NUMBER: 58–5187. DIS-
TRIBUTED IN CANADA BY AMBASSADOR BOOKS, LTD., TORONTO. THE DRAWINGS FOR THIS BOOK WERE
DRAWN DIRECTLY ON STONE BY THE ARTIST AND THE BOOK WAS LITHOGRAPHED IN FOUR COLORS BY
GEORGE C. MILLER AND SON OF NEW YORK, IN THE UNITED STATES OF AMERICA. THE FIRST STANZA
OF "THE CREMATION OF SAM MCGEE" IS REPRINTED FROM *The Collected Works of Robert Service*
BY PERMISSION OF DODD, MEAD AND COMPANY.

CONTENTS

CHAPTER I   SHIELD OF THE NORTH

ACROSS THE upper half of the continent of North America, between
the spread-out fingers of the Great Lakes and the wide curve of Hudson
Bay, lies a huge shield of the oldest rock in the world. Glaciers moved
along it in the ice age, leaving thousands of cold lakes and streams, from
the Laurentian Mountains in the east to the high Rockies in the west.
Powerful rivers flow north to the Arctic Sea, east to the Atlantic and
west to the Pacific. Canada is a land of forest and water. Salt waters
of the Atlantic sweep along fog-clouded Labrador and fruitful Nova
Scotia, and on the Pacific Ocean Vancouver Island is like a small re-
minder of old England.

    In the west is wheat and cattle country—the plains where herds of
buffalo once thundered over the grasses—while to the north the North-

west Territory and the Yukon lie white and cold under the midnight sun for many months of the year. Around the Great Lakes, farms have taken the place of forest, and throughout Canada the ancient rocks have given up gold, silver, iron, copper and other minerals.

In the year 1000 A.D. Leif Ericson, son of Eric the Red, ventured westward from Iceland and Greenland, and came ashore on some unknown spot on the coast of New England or Canada. He and his men called the land Vinland, for the wild grapes that were growing there. Some think that Vikings may have come also through the straits into Hudson Bay, and down to the Great Lakes; for swords, spears, and fire-steel thought to be of Norse origin have been found. In that region a stone, carved with writing of the fourteenth century, was discovered, suggesting that the Viking Sea Wolves may have made a settlement inland. Legend has it that the first white child born in North America was Snorre, a Viking. Then the Vikings stopped coming, and no trace of a settlement remained.

Several hundred years later, on a July day in 1534, Captain Jacques Cartier, flinging his plain brown cloak back from his shoulders, looked up at the thirty-foot cross being erected by his crew. Earth, forest and sky, newly washed by storms, glistened in hot sunlight. The calm captain glanced behind him warily at a crowd of Indians held back by awe of the white men in colored clothing, and by fear of the muskets in their hands, and of the black cannons on ships swinging at anchor in the river. The cross stood straight at last, made crudely of the native trees of New France, cut with the fleur-de-lis, and surmounted by a carved wooden

shield, proclaiming: *"Vive le roi de France."* Cartier and his men, hands
on their weapons, dropped to their knees in prayer. When they arose
and returned to their ships they were followed by a swift fleet of canoes
filled with Indians who feared them as gods, yet suspected them as devils.

The captain had come searching for the "Northwest Passage" to the
jeweled Orient. He was not the first to hunt this mythical passage, and
to reach this northern land. John Cabot, a roving Italian who became an
Englishman, had sailed his small ship, the *Matthew*, to the shores of
Newfoundland in 1497, just five years after Columbus had set foot in
the West Indies. Cabot claimed this shore for England, but he did not
venture into the broad inland river. England failed to follow up Cabot's
discovery and sent no expeditions to colonize. Yet the salty men of
England, as well as of France and Portugal, ventured across the Atlantic
to the banks of Newfoundland, and started fishing expeditions that have
continued until today.

Now Jacques Cartier, on this day in July, listened to unknown Indian
words without understanding, but he understood well enough when
two young braves, sons of the Indian king, pointed to gold and jeweled
ornaments worn by some of the seamen, and then to the north across
the river.

"Saguenay," they said, and the sea captain believed that they meant
that in a country to the northwest there was a land of that name, where
golden treasure could be found. He invited the braves to board his ship
and return to France with him. The stories these Indians told with ges-
tures and halting French so fired the greed of the French king that he

sent Cartier on a second voyage. The shrewd captain sailed up the St. Lawrence, landed at Quebec's high rock with the Indian village of Stadacona at its foot, and after spending two weeks there went on up the river to an island. Here there was a large town, called Hochelaga, enclosed by a wooden palisade, surrounded by green fields where corn grew. A mountain behind the town blazed with autumn colors, and Cartier named the summit Mont Royal. His farther advance was barred by the river's fast rapids, so he returned to Stadacona for the winter. Nearby he built two small wooden forts. Cartier found no gold or jewels, and the Northwest Passage remained a dream that continued to beckon other men across the seas. He listened to the Indians speaking of a vast country stretching endlessly beyond great waterfalls and rivers, but he did not see it.

In the spring Cartier set sail for France, disappointed. He was unaware of the great resources that would make Canada a nation—its rocks, its soil, its animals and forests, its powerful rivers and thousands of lakes.

CHAPTER II   HIAWATHA'S PEOPLE

THE INDIANS who watched the small caravels of Cartier spread sails for France were members of the Algonquin speaking peoples living along the St. Lawrence and north of the Great Lakes. Around camp fires in summer, when the loon called his lonely cry, and in huts buried in snows in winter, grandmothers told children of the young Hiawatha, who had been the friend of Adjidauma, the chattering squirrel, and of Owaissa, the bluebird. As the boys grew taller older warriors of the village gave them their first bows and spoke to them of Hiawatha, the young hunter, and of how he killed the red deer with one swift flight of an arrow. Women said that it was Hiawatha who had taught their mothers to grow green corn, placing in their hands the seeds that pushed up from the earth in tasseled stalks, and that he gave them yellow squash to creep along the rows of corn. Medicine men, doing wild dances with painted faces and horns of moose and deer on their heads, claimed that Hiawatha gave them their herbs and magic.

When gods of the frozen winter unlocked streams from the ice, the Indian boy heard the tale of how Hiawatha taught his people to make a swift canoe of bent saplings of green cedar, covered with birchbark, sealed with gummy pitch of the spruce tree.

The little Ojibway girl, weaving a woodland sash of buffalo wool, dyed bright blue or red by juice of bark and berries, sang to herself the story of the wooing of Hiawatha and Minnehaha, as she looked now and then to see how her baby brother swung, wrapped to his papoose board, on the branch of a pine tree.

The Ojibways lived in the forests along the shores of the Great Lakes. To the north were the Ottawas, and in the east, on the peninsula made by the St. Lawrence, with Lakes Erie, Ontario and Huron, the large Huron tribe had many settled villages. The Algonquin speaking people put down in picture form, on sacred rolls of birchbark, something of their religion and their ways, and they said that it was Hiawatha, coming down to them from the happy hunting grounds in the sky, who told them to do this.

Although the people of the forests and lakes grew a small amount of corn and squash, they lived mainly by hunting and fishing. They moved about in families or small groups, covering long stretches of woodland. The animals that they killed for food and clothing, and for pelts to trade to the white men, were never found in large numbers. The forest Indians seldom had a great deal to eat, and often went hungry when game grew scarce.

However, there were usually a few good seasons of the year for food. In the early spring Ojibways and others in the lake regions went to the maple groves. There they made sugar and feasted on it until they grew fat. When wild rice ripened they pushed their light canoes among the shallow swamps and gathered rice for their cooking pots. At the St. Mary's rapids, where lakes Superior and Huron come together, Indian tribes gathered to spear white fish and hang them on long poles and racks to dry for winter use.

Enemies of the Algonquin peoples were the Five Nations, later called the Six Nations when the Tuscaroras came up from the south to join the confederacy. These tribes were the Mohawks, Senecas, Cayugas, Onondagas and Oneidas, and together they were called the Iroquois. They were known also as the People of the Long House, since their palisaded villages were made up of long houses, where families lived together. The red man called Hiawatha was thought to be a great leader of the Onondaga tribe of the Iroquois. The Iroquois also claimed Hiawatha as their hero and prophet, yet he had told them nothing of the white-skinned strangers.

For seventy-five years after Cartier these strange white men did not return. Then, one day Samuel de Champlain landed beneath the great rock, near the spot where the village of Stadacona had once stood, and had his men build a little wooden fort, calling it Quebec. The Hurons, Ottawas, and Montaignas made friends with these powerful white men, and brought them furs and meat from the forest.

CHAPTER III FATHER OF NEW FRANCE

CARTIER'S tiny log buildings near Stadacona had fallen in ruins, but the small fort of Quebec stood under a huge dome of rock that was a fortress in itself. Champlain saw this spot on the river as the best place for defense against hostile Indians, and as a center for a settlement. Champlain, the son of a hardy sea captain, was also member of a family that belonged to the lesser nobility in France. He had made several previous voyages to Canada, and had spent a winter at the fort of Port Royal in Nova Scotia. He was fired with an imagination that Cartier lacked, and he was a man who could understand the Indian and the vast unknown land. Champlain knew that France could stay here only by settlement. In 1608 he brought a small colony to settle around the Quebec fort, and to cut farms from the dark forest above the great rock.

On a June morning, in 1609, a fleet of canoes skimmed over the river in early mists, led by a boat in which Champlain sat with some of his men. This exploring expedition went up the river, as far as the wooded Thousand Islands. On the return, when Champlain saw the mouth of the Richelieu River, he gave an order to two of his men to accompany him with the Indians in several canoes. The excited Hurons made it known that this river led south into enemy Iroquois country, but they were persuaded to go along in spite of their fears.

The canoes, pushing swiftly up the river, came out into a large lake, later to be called Lake Champlain, and then into a smaller body of water, Lake George. Here the Hurons pointed fearfully to distant elm bark canoes, indicating that they were manned by Iroquois. Shouting insults the Iroquois moved back to shore, and all that night they danced war dances around their camp fires. The Huron canoes kept together out on the lake, but at dawn Champlain commanded them to go ashore.

As the Iroquois advanced to meet them, led by three chieftains, the quaking Hurons, with Champlain in the center and a white soldier on either side, though hidden behind the Indians, moved suddenly forward. Overcome with awe at their first sight of a bearded, fair-skinned man, the chiefs stood still. Raising his arquebus, Champlain killed the three chieftains. The Iroquois, although stiff with fear of this "white god" and his terrible fire and explosion, realized that they must fight for their lives. As they loosed a flight of arrows, the other two soldiers stepped forward and fired. At this the Iroquois turned and ran for the woods, and the Hurons moved on the wounded to scalp and kill.

Next morning Champlain and his men started their return in the Huron canoes to Quebec. Champlain made two more voyages of exploration, one part way up the Ottawa River, and the other to Georgian Bay. His astrolabe, an instrument for taking observations from the sun's position, was found a long time after not far from the Ottawa River. Then for some years he had no more time for exploration, for his small colony of sixty-five men and women was in grave difficulties. France sent no money to them, and too many of the first colonists were criminals and outcasts who did no work, spending their time drinking, gambling and fighting, when they were not roaming the woods trading brandy to the Indians for furs.

Nevertheless the colony endured, and news of this rich farm land had spread in France. In 1617 Louis Hébert, the first *habitant*, as the French Canadian farmer was called, arrived with his wife and two small daughters. Oddly enough, he had not been a farmer in France, but was an

adventurous apothecary and physician from Paris. He cut the tall trees, built a stone house and barn, and grew his crops on the crest of the rock of Quebec. Hébert brought the first ox to Canada, to plow his twelve acres. The company which financed the colony had given Hébert hard terms to meet, but he and his wife and daughters worked in the fields and made a farm that prospered. On a sunny crisp morning Champlain himself liked to climb the steep path from the governor's house to the top to have a talk with Hébert. The habitant's daughters married after a while; one did not live long, but the other raised a large family as strong as their grandparents. In 1627 Hébert died from injuries received in a fall, and Madame Hébert took over the farm work and ran the place well for many years.

Although Champlain knew that the affairs of the settlement had to come first, still he, like his fellows, never gave up his liking for exploration. His companion in many voyages up the streams into unknown country was Étienne Brulé, tall, strong and venturesome. Brulé liked the life of the woods so well that he became almost like an Indian himself. He married into a tribe, learned several Indian languages, and went far out into the wilderness. He was the first white actually to live with Indians, and he left no records. How Brulé died, or why, has never been known exactly, but his end came in the forests, and people in Quebec heard that he had been killed by Indians.

The northern tribes were always friendly to the French, while the Five Nations smoldered with rage at the white men for Champlain's attack on them on Lake George. This first battle set the stage for a hatred of the French that never left the People of the Long House, and that was, many years later, to make them allies of the English.

CHAPTER IV   THE DISCOVERY

At a time when the French, under Champlain, were discovering rivers
and lakes in New France, an Englishman, Captain Henry Hudson, was
searching for the fabulous Northwest Passage to China. He sailed up
the Hudson River past a small island called Manhattan, and then came
down again, disappointed.

In 1611 he ventured once more in his ship, the *Discovery*, through
far northern waters, where an icy current swung the small vessel along
between high cliffs. On the deck Hudson stared straight before him, con-
fident that he had at last found the water passage to the Orient. Others
had been as far as this strait, but no one had gone beyond it.

As he came out into a huge bay the red-haired captain's eyes gleamed,
and he smiled at his son, who stood beside him. Surely this water must

lead to China! For three months the *Discovery* sailed along the shores of Hudson Bay, and, as snow began to fall, it anchored in a smaller body of water now called James Bay. Ice thickened around the ship, and snow came in blizzards that shook the masts and drove the crew below. Scurvy, a disease caused by lack of fresh food, struck down the men.

When spring came at last, some had died and others were fighting among themselves. Most of their hatred turned on Hudson, who had filled them with dreams of the rich eastern lands that they now knew could not be found here, and had brought them to this desolate country. Even when Hudson agreed to return to England they hated him. Before the *Discovery* could set sail Hudson fell into a violent argument with a young sailor. As the captain stood on deck, his long red hair flying in the cold wind, he and his son, with a few loyal men, were taken from behind and put ashore. The mutineers set sail for home. Later, on a wild coast where they landed to hunt for fresh meat, they were set upon and some killed by Eskimos. When the *Discovery* finally made port in England the survivors were thrown into prison for mutiny on the high seas.

Nobody knows what happened to Henry Hudson and his young son. There are legendary tales in the north about red-haired Indians who live near Hudson Bay, and some people believe that perhaps the small band of white men were taken into a Cree Indian tribe, where they married and lived out their lives. The tragic end of the voyage of the *Discovery* marks the end also of the search for the Northwest Passage in the early days by the English.

CHAPTER V   THE ROCK OF QUEBEC

THE DEATH of Champlain in 1635 cast a gloom over Quebec, but the following year, when a new governor arrived, everybody came down to welcome him. The Hébert farm was not the only one now along the river, and the largest of these new holdings was that of Sieur Giffard, who had brought the ancient landed estate system of the old country to the New World.

Giffard received his lands from the king of France, and then he let farms out to men who paid him both in money and in produce. He had come as a ship's doctor, as well as a local magistrate, and he owned the only flour mill. His mill must grind for all of the farms on his land, and

his rents were so small that he often gave out more in traditional feasts than he received. On May 1 his tenants brought in a tree, decorated with ribbons, and planted it to the music of drum and horn before the manor house. Then the farmers trooped inside and were treated to a feast.

For thirty-three years the tiny town of Quebec with its nearby farms and little mission post a few miles away was the only settlement. Each summer ships dropped anchors beneath the high rock, and from them came courageous men and women—farmers, soldiers, tradesmen, members of religious orders. Among the latter was Mother Marie de l'Incarnation, a patient, steadfast worker, first Superior of the new Ursuline Convent.

Mother Marie taught school in the convent for the children of the settlers at Quebec, and on every fine afternoon she gathered Indian children about her under a spreading ash tree nearby. She understood that they belonged to the forest, and so she had them sit around her on the grass in their buckskin clothing. As she taught them she learned their languages, and after a while was able to speak to them in Huron, Algonquin and even in Iroquois.

One of the young priests watched the small group, and when the children had gone he asked Mother Marie, as she took up her books to return to the convent building, "Why do you allow them to wear savage clothing? Why don't you bring them indoors and civilize them?"

Mother Marie said quietly, "They must see the woods. Loss of freedom makes them sad, and sadness makes them ill."

The convent nuns and the sisters of the hospital, the Hôtel Dieu, had duties quite unlike those they had known in France. At a moment's notice they must leave their prayers to fight fires that often swept through the wooden buildings, or to nurse the sick in time of epidemic, or load muskets when the dreaded Iroquois attacked.

When Maisonneuve, in 1641, brought a colony to settle the island upriver where Mont Royal raised its wooded top, two nuns came with the party. They were Jeanne Mance and Marguerite Bourgeoys. Montreal, as the name became, was even more dangerous a spot than Quebec, for it was closer to Iroquois country. The city was founded as a mission, growing into a frontier town that became the center of the fur trade. As time passed, farms were cut out of the forests along the river on both sides. A third town, Three Rivers, sprang up around a log fort where the junction of two streams and the St. Lawrence came together between Montreal and Quebec.

CHAPTER VI   BLACK GOWNS

MEN FROM the settlements were going out in ever greater numbers to
live with the Indians. Along with them went the Jesuit priests. They
tucked their robes about their legs in birchbark canoes, or walked tire-
lessly through the bush, carrying the cross of the Catholic church to
brown-skinned men and women. Some of these "black gowns" became
explorers while others founded missions among friendly tribes.

The Hurons had always been the most settled of the tribes of Canada,
and the most agricultural, although they followed the Indian custom
of moving on to new land when fields had been used a few summers.
The Hurons were most friendly to the "black gowns." By 1648 the
Jesuits had a dozen well-built missions in villages in the fertile stretch
of land between Lakes Huron and Simcoe. Here Father Daniel, Father
Brébeuf and Father Lalemont encouraged the Indians to make permanent
gardens and orchards around small log-walled villages.

Then came the terrible July day, when Father Daniel was killed by
an arrow as he conducted Mass, and Iroquois attackers massacred the
people and burned the village of St. Joseph.

After this victory the Iroquois went back to their own territory near

Lake Erie and for a time the missions were left in peace. The Hurons did not expect another attack before spring, but in March, with snow thickly carpeting the earth and hanging heavy on the trees, the Iroquois came again.

The strongest fort was Ste. Marie, and two smaller missions, St. Ignace and St. Louis, were close enought to it to feel protected. Father Brébeuf and Father Lalemont had just gone to St. Ignace from Ste. Marie when an exhausted runner came with news that St. Louis had been attacked and destroyed and that the Iroquois were advancing on St. Ignace. Brébeuf was a strong man, much admired by the Indians because he could carry a canoe or a heavy pack, or paddle all day with the best of the Hurons. Lalemont was quite small and thin. Brébeuf looked anxiously at his companion, asking, "Shall we return at once to Ste. Marie? It is only eight miles away, and I believe that we can make it."

"No," said Lalemont calmly. "You and I could make it, but these people could not get there in time with us. We must stay."

They did not have long to wait. As the terrible war cry of the Iroquois burst on their ears the attackers were already swarming over the palisaded walls. The priests watched helplessly as men, women and children were scalped and killed, and the village rang with cries and groans. Father Brébeuf had a strange feeling that this had happened to him before, and then he remembered a dream that had come to him long ago. In his sleep he seemed to see these same enemies killing people. He recalled the next scene in his dream—one in which he was carried to a wooden stake and tortured, with flames rising around him. It was in that way that he died on this hot Sunday morning in the Huron village. Mercifully he died quickly, but frail little Father Lalemont lived on for eleven terrible hours before he was killed.

Yet other priests came, some to live and work with the Indians, and others to die at their hands. Forts were destroyed, and the fields and villages of the Hurons were all put to the torch. The best work of the Jesuits was wiped out, and the Huron tribe scattered. Many went to an island in Georgian Bay, but most of them came back because there was not enough game there to feed them. Others went westward to join the Ojibways, and the large Huron nation was never again prosperous and settled. Yet priests continued to push out into the wilderness, to found missions, and to explore the rivers. Like the men of the settlements— Quebec, Three Rivers and Montreal—they refused to stay within town walls where they could have led safe and quiet lives.

CHAPTER VII LORD GOOSEBERRY AND THE LITTLE DEVIL

"No, Mr. Gooseberry, you and your brother-in-law, Radisson, will not be granted permission to go furring among the Indians unless you take two of my friends, and share the profits."

Groseillers and Radisson stood before the haughty beribboned governor in the Citadel of St. Louis on Cape Diamond, as the crest of the rock at Quebec was called. No one but austere Bishop Laval of the Jesuits could contradict the governor, even though the citizens of Montreal disliked him heartily and paid very little attention to his orders.

Groseillers, which meant gooseberries, was the joking nickname given to Médart Chouart by the rowdy men of Three Rivers, because the land owned by Chouart was called "The Gooseberry Patch." But the "Lord of the Gooseberry Patch" didn't care. His wife took charge of their farm and managed the large family of children, and as for him—the wild life of the forests suited him much better. He traded for furs with the Indians, and traveled always with his young brother-in-law, Pierre Radisson. The two men bowed mockingly to the governor of New France and sauntered out, down the winding street into the lower town at the foot of the rock, where they embarked in their canoe.

Early next day, before the sun was above the broad St. Lawrence River, so early that only a few wisps of smoke were rising from chimneys on the small peaked roofs of Three Rivers, two men slipped silently out past guards at the log walls. These men wore buckskin clothing, with the white knit caps of their town, and they were bent under loads of gear, as they headed toward the St. Maurice River. Governor or no governor, Groseillers and Radisson were off into the tall forests of the unknown continent of North America for a year or two.

How could laws made by the king of France control these *coureurs de bois,* or "runners of the woods"? As a child Radisson had been captured by the Mohawks and had lived with them for several years. The Mohawks called him the "Little Devil." He and Groseillers knew the Indians and the forests, lakes and rivers, better than any white men of their time. They understood many things that other Frenchmen did not know. They knew that it was possible to reach wide, mysterious Hudson Bay by a network of lakes and rivers, instead of going around by the long sea route to the north. They knew that a vast wealth of furs lay in the region.

Two years later, when Radisson and Groseillers came paddling back down the rivers with a fleet of canoes laden with a fortune in furs, roaring their French *voyageur* songs, they were met by officers who took away most of the load. Radisson and Groseillers, after futile protests to the king of France, went to England. There they reached the ear of King Charles II, who had just come to the throne after the defeat of the Roundheads and the death of Oliver Cromwell. They told the king that England could do well with the trade in furs, if only she could get a foothold at Hudson Bay. A group of nobles and merchants headed by Prince Rupert came together to form "The Governor and Company of Adventurers of England Trading into Hudson Bay." This was the beginning of the celebrated Hudson's Bay Company. The "Lord of the Gooseberry Patch" and the "Little Devil," however, never got any more money out of it than they had been able to get from their furring adventures out of Three Rivers.

CHAPTER VIII

HERE THEY STOOD!

BEHIND THE walls of the little town of Montreal men kept their guns handy and women went about their work with pale faces and a careful eye on their children. Hunters had been in with the terrible news that the Iroquois were gathering on the Ottawa River in large numbers—some said that as many as a thousand warriors were encamped there. Friendly Indians had told them that the Men of the Long House were wearing war paint, and that war dances were being held. It looked as if the Iroquois were about to launch a campaign to destroy Montreal.

A grave council discussed this news, but there seemed to be nothing to do except to stay within the town walls and take every means for defense. Maisonneuve, the founder of Montreal, and Charles Le Moyne, their most experienced citizen, felt that this crisis might be the final one for the settlement. Then Adam Dollard came in. Dollard was a twenty-five-year-old army officer who had lived in New France for three years. He had a plan.

"I will take a small group of volunteers, go up the Ottawa River, and intercept the first band of warriors coming down. This will probably be a hunting party, and if we kill them all the news may stop an attack on Montreal. We will take them by surprise."

Le Moyne frowned and turned to Maisonneuve, "This might work, but we do not know how many Iroquois are on the river. It is very dangerous."

Maisonneuve nodded. "It is too dangerous for such a small party."

But Dollard would not give up his plan, and when sixteen men offered to go with him, no move was made to stop him.

Next day Dollard and his men paddled up the Ottawa River, portaging around several rapids, and finally came to a place thirty miles upstream where they decided to ambush the first canoes of the Iroquois. This was a spot called the Long Sault, named for the rapids that churned through a narrow passage between high banks. The dark forest

was silent, and the men could hear nothing but the sound of the rapids. On the bank was an old stockade made of logs, once used by Indians. Near it the Frenchmen waited in the undergrowth. They had scarcely taken up position when a group of friendly Hurons and Algonquins appeared to join them. Dollard now had sixteen French and forty-four Indians under his command.

There they waited patiently for several days, and then suddenly several canoes came swinging down the stream. When the Iroquois pulled in to shore and landed, the attackers opened fire and cut them down. One brave escaped, and made his way upriver on foot to warn his party. As the Frenchmen and their allies were reloading, down the river shot a fleet of fifty canoes filled with Iroquois.

"Take cover!" shouted Dollard, and his men made for the stockade. As the howling Iroquois rushed them the men inside met the onslaught with killing fire. The Iroquois retreated to the forest for a pow-wow, and then sent a few braves forward to talk. Several Frenchmen fired, killing the emissaries. The Huron chief shook his head, saying to Dollard,

"Friend, you should have listened to their words. Now we die."

For ten days Dollard and his men held out. During this time the

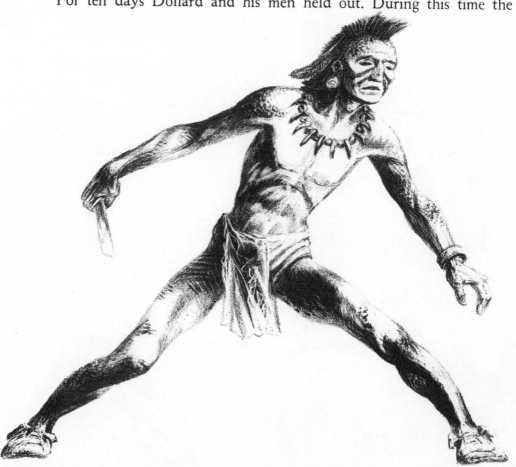

Iroquois kept calling to the Indians within the stockade to come over to them, and, one by one, they crept out to join the enemy. At last the Huron chief was the only Indian left. On the fifth day five hundred more Iroquois came to the attack. Still the few men behind the low log barricade held out, although they were almost dead of thirst. The earth around them was covered with Iroquois dead. As the final assault began, and the Indians hurled burning torches into the stockade, Dollard loaded his musketoon like a bomb, and attempted to throw it out among the enemy. It exploded before it went over and killed several of the men inside. At this the Iroquois rushed in with their tomahawks, and the battle was over.

All of New France honored this heroic little band, for their stand saved Montreal, and probably Three Rivers and Quebec as well. The warriors of the Five Nations, awed by the bravery of Dollard and his men, decided that if so small a group could kill so many of the invincible Iroquois, then it would be wiser not to learn what a larger defense force could do.

CHAPTER IX   TOOLS, SEEDS AND LOOMS

THE WHOLE town of Quebec turned out in holiday dress to welcome a new governor. This was autumn, in 1665, and scarlet, orange and yellow foliage were not more brilliant than the petticoats, jackets, sashes and caps of the citizens. Drummers and pipers preceded the retiring governor as he came from the Chateau of St. Louis on the rock, and walked down the curving path in his satins, and plumed hat, sword clanking against a lordly leg. With him came black-robed Bishop Laval, of the stern face, and a group of priests and nuns.

When the first ship docked, down the gangplank tottered a sick Governor Courcelle, making a poor entrance after a long and exceptionally rough voyage. Behind him was Jean Talon, the first *intendant*, or manager, of the business affairs of New France. Passengers were so ill that many had to be taken to the already overcrowded hospital, and others bedded down on the floors of homes jammed with sick arrivals from previous ships. The famous Carignan Regiment, first regular troops to be sent to the colony, was coming in detachments on every ship, and the troops had to be housed also.

These soldiers, veterans of the Turkish wars, were welcomed heartily in Quebec, for it was believed that now the Iroquois would be defeated. On board ship with the first arrivals was a giant of a priest, Father Dollier de Casson, a man so tall and strong that he was called the "Samson of New France." When Father Dollier went with the regiment down into Iroquois country, and two enemy warriors crept up on him from behind, he turned, caught them and cracked their heads together so hard that the sound was heard for nearly a mile—or so it was said.

This expedition against the Iroquois was undertaken by the new governor in midwinter, against the advice of woodsmen. There were few cheers from the men of the colony as the governor marched out at the head of the troops in their gray uniforms and purple stockings. They were not surprised when the troops returned from an unsuccessful campaign, one in which many troopers died, and the return was made with the aid of the woodsmen who went with them. Nevertheless the glitter of uniforms in rows and of muskets impressed the Iroquois and caused them to make peace.

Meanwhile the plump new intendant was kept busy attending to the many problems of the colony. When Jean Talon had trouble getting money from France he set about finding ways to make the colony more independent. He started a ship-building plant, a tannery and a brewery. He brought over shopkeepers, as well as workers in hand industries. He gave out strips of land to settlers who promised to clear them and make farms. And he had seeds sent out, and farm animals imported, including sheep. It was Talon who gave the first looms to the women of Quebec and Montreal.

More settlers were needed, and there were not enough wives in New France. Talon got up a scheme to bring girls over from farms and convent schools in France. These were called "the King's Girls," since the Crown paid for their passage, and they were married almost as soon as they stepped off the ship in Quebec. Later other shiploads of wives were brought, and Talon wrote to the king the following year that the plan had worked well, for already most of the wives had children.

Talon believed firmly in exploration for the glory of France. He sent the Sieur du Lhut out into the west, and there this "King of the Woodsmen" built forts, established fur-trading posts, and brought about peace between the warlike tribes of the Sioux and the Assiniboines. He founded the fort of Detroit, and manned it with coureurs de bois. The city of Duluth is named for him. When a twenty-year peace pact was signed with the Five Nations, Talon sent other explorers farther out into the

west, to claim lands for France. But the governor had friends in the French royal court who persuaded the king to recall Talon. When Jean Talon left New France after three years it was, because of his great ability, a stronger and more prosperous colony than it had ever been before.

CHAPTER X   THE GREAT RIVER

KING LOUIS, strutting about his palaces in France, was annoyed at his colony in the New World because the men had a way of wandering instead of plowing the earth and keeping shop. Too many of them joined Indian tribes, or lived among them as traders and returned to smuggle pelts illegally into Montreal and Quebec, to be shipped to Europe in vessels made with secret compartments. The king could not collect his furring taxes. And even the Jesuits left their far-flung mission stations to go exploring.

The towns were full of tales of huge buffalo herds, of strange tribes in the west, and of unknown mighty rivers. A young priest, Jacques Marquette, hearing these stories, felt that he must explore these rivers. Accompanied by an expert woodsman, Louis Joliet, they left the mission of St. Ignace at the head of Lake Michigan one May morning in 1672 and embarked in two canoes. They had with them five Indians.

Louis Joliet had been born in Canada, the son of a poor wagon maker, who had come to Port Royal in Nova Scotia, from France. Joliet had given up training for the priesthood to become a fur trader. When Father Marquette founded the small mission he was filled with religious zeal, but as he listened to the stories told by wandering Indians, he knew that he could not rest until he saw these distant places, where no white man had ever been. He learned several Indian languages, and he heard that a mighty stream called the Mississippi, or Father of Waters, flowed southward. Perhaps this was the mysterious Northwest Passage? Who could tell?

The canoes skimmed swiftly along the shore of the big lake, through rivers and smaller lakes, into the lands of the Miamis and of the Kicka-poos. From the Wisconsin they floated into a wide muddy river, moving southward. The Indian paddlers pointed, with fear of the unknown in their eyes.

"This is the Father of Waters! The great river."

Birds were nesting thickly on the banks, and swimming on the water. Marquette and Joliet believed that theirs were the first foreign eyes to see the river. They continued to the mouth of the Arkansas, and then turned back upstream. Marquette knew now that this was not the passage to the Orient, but that here a vast domain could be claimed for the King of France.

He returned to his mission at St. Ignace, while Joliet went on to Quebec. As Joliet's canoes ran the Lachine Rapids in the St. Lawrence near Montreal, one overturned, drowning two men and losing the careful report of their journey Marquette had prepared. The canoemen had been down forty-two rapids on their long trip without mishap, only to meet disaster as they reached the end. Father Marquette, on hearing of this, patiently wrote another account of the voyage, and sent it on to Quebec. A few years later, the little priest died while on a journey to the Illinois country to found another mission. He was buried by the Michigan river that bears his name.

WHEN THE Comte de Frontenac arrived in Canada people had grown weary of weak officials. "After all," they shrugged, "we have not had a strong governor since Champlain." Nobody expected another Champlain, for who could be the equal of the Father of New France? Before much time had passed they were to discover, however, that the Comte de Frontenac was strong, and, more than that, he was a man whom the Indians liked and respected. He became known as the Lion of New France.

The first and most serious problem facing the new governor was the Iroquois danger. Although the twenty-year peace treaty signed with the Five Nations held off a real war, it was no help against frequent small forays. The tribes did not regard such an attack by a few braves as breaking the peace treaty.

As his first act, then, Frontenac called a big pow-wow at Cataraqui, on the St. Lawrence River above Montreal. As the Indians watched silently from the shore they saw a boat approaching, with the haughty governor, in silken clothing and plumed hat, sitting in an armchair in the bow. Over him was spread a silk canopy embroidered with the fleur-de-lis' of France.

Behind Frontenac, as he stepped ashore, came officers with their swords and shining breast plates catching the sun, and then a fleet of canoes swept in to land men in buckskin, wearing the red caps of Quebec, the blue of Montreal, and the white of Three Rivers. Opposite the French the Indian chiefs were seated, impressed by the grandeur. To them the white standard was the color of peace. They had not before seen an *onontio*, or father, like this one. With him they smoked the peace pipe and promised no harm to the white men. They watched in astonishment as a log fort with strong palisades, called Fort Frontenac, was built there in four days. And then they were even more surprised when the new governor took off his sword and hat to join them singing and dancing

around the camp fire. Here was a man the Indians could understand!

For Frontenac peace with the Indians was the first step in his dream of empire on the North American continent. In René Cavelier, the Sieur de La Salle, who had been in the colony six years when Frontenac arrived, he found a man who shared that dream.

La Salle, small and thin, with a sharp dark face, possessed imagination and daring beyond that of any other explorer of New France. He had left the Jesuit order and come to the new world when he was twenty-four years old. Like so many others he believed that he was born to find the Northwest Passage to China, and he called his land outside Montreal La Chine. The name became Lachine, and the name was also given to the great rapids nearby in the St. Lawrence.

When his restless spirit could no longer be kept in check, La Salle sold his property and went west, where he wandered for two years. On his return and in company with his lifelong friend, Tonty, he was then sent by Frontenac to take charge of Fort Frontenac. This Henry Tonty, son of an Italian nobleman, had lost his right hand in a sea battle, and had replaced it with an iron hand. It was said that he could handle a sword as skillfully with the iron hand as another man could with a real one.

To bring furs in quantity from the west La Salle built a ship on the river above Niagara Falls. The forty-five foot vessel called the *Griffin* was launched when spring melted the ice. As Indians watched, frightened —for they thought it a magical monster—the *Griffin* sailed out into Lake Erie, on into Lake Huron, and then down Lake Michigan. Staying on at the head of the lakes, La Salle and Tonty sent the ship back without them, loaded with pelts. The little vessel did not arrive. Its fate has never been known for certain. Somehow it must have foundered and sunk, with all on board lost.

In 1681 La Salle and Tonty, with twenty-three French and a fleet of canoes manned by Indians, left Fort Heartbreak on the Illinois River and paddled to the mouth of the Mississippi, claiming all lands for France. Some years later La Salle took a small colony from France across the ocean to the Mississippi. The ship landed on the coast of Texas instead, and La Salle went with a little group of men to find the Mississippi. There on the shore of the wide river he was killed by his mutinous men.

In Quebec Frontenac was in a constant struggle with stern Bishop Laval, who wanted to make the entire colony a Jesuit mission. The bishop tried to stop the trading of brandy to Indians, and wanted the license

law for the fur trade enforced. But the wild coureurs de bois paid no attention to the laws.

Frontenac was wise enough to know that such laws could not be enforced. After six years in New France the "arrogant soldier," as the Jesuits called him, was called home in disgrace. During the next years two new governors failed to keep peace with the Five Nations. At last the king understood that he had only one man who could do this. At seventy-six years of age the old Lion was asked to return to New France.

Frontenac found the Indians on the war path, and the English in the colonies to the south angry because the previous governor had built a fort at Niagara to corner the fur trade. Frontenac immediately launched a campaign against both the Five Nation Iroquois and the English. Reckless woodsmen joined French troops in a fast series of forays, in which they killed the people of several villages in New York and New England and left their homes smoking ruins. The English, in retaliation, organized a naval expedition to attack New France. They took Port Royal, and then all of Acadia, and after that victory they sailed up the St. Lawrence with thirty-two vessels to besiege Quebec.

The city was weakly defended and old Frontenac was weary. On his last campaign he had been carried over the portages in a chair. But he was as resolute and cunning as ever. He fooled the English into thinking that Quebec was filled with fighting men and guns, and so the English fleet sailed away without a major battle. The following year the Comte de Frontenac died in the Chateau of St. Louis, and was buried, by his own wishes, not in the Jesuit cathedral, but in the little chapel of the Récollet monks who had been his friends.

CHAPTER XII

ACROSS THE St. Lawrence River from the island of Montreal was the estate of a *seigneur* of New France, Charles Le Moyne. This old man, who had fought Indians in the wars many times, took part in the councils of the colony with no less energy than he governed his tenant farmers. He had a family of eleven remarkable sons.

Although Le Moyne was their family name, the sons took other names to distinguish one from another. The oldest remained Charles Le Moyne, inheritor of the finest manor house and farms in Canada. Charles was a man of good judgment and courage. His brother, Pierre Le Moyne d'Iberville was a leader in Indian fighting and a commander on the sea. He died in Cuba on his way to found the city of New Orleans, a task left to his brother, Jean Bienville, who had accompanied him.

The other brothers were as much at home in the woods and with the Indians as were these three. One of them, Paul, was called "Little-Bird-Always-In-Motion" by his Indian friends, and it was he who so often helped make peace with the tribes. Another brother was Louis Le Moyne de Chateauguay, who was killed storming the English Hudson's Bay Company posts in 1686. England and France were at peace, yet the growing fur trade out of Hudson Bay brought skirmishes between the English and French fur traders.

The exploits of these brothers were so fabulous as to sound like legend, even while their adventures were making living history in the new world.

CHAPTER XIII

ON A WARM DAY of Indian summer Madeleine de Verchères, fourteen and a half years old, sat on the small log dock and swung her feet over the water of the St. Lawrence River. Most of the men and women who lived within the safety of Fort Verchères were in the fields nearby, gathering a good harvest of squash, corn and pumpkin. Madeleine could hear their voices, calling or raised in song. She would have liked to have

gone to Montreal with her mother, who would be there several days,
or to Quebec where her father, an officer in the Carignan Regiment and
commander of the fort, had gone on army business. Near her sat Laviolette, an old man who worked for her father, mending his fishing net.

A burst of gunfire shattered the peaceful autumn day. Laviolette
sprang up, shouting,

"Mademoiselle, run for the fort. The Iroquois!"

Already Madeleine could hear two women crying out that the Iroquois
had killed their husbands. Madeleine and Laviolette pulled them into
the gateway and swung the big door closed. Then Madeleine ran through
the covered passageway from the fort into the blockhouse. Here she saw
one of the two soldiers on duty there just about to fling a blazing torch
into some kegs of gunpowder.

"Stop! What are you doing?"

"We'll have to blow up the fort. We are surrounded by Iroquois.
Listen!"

Madeleine pushed him away, and grasping the torch she stamped it
out on the floor. "Get to your muskets! We can hold out." Her voice
was suddenly like her father's, stern and commanding. The soldier stiff-
ened and obeyed. Madeleine ran from one firing point to the next, shouting orders, putting the older women to work loading guns, sending the
three men and some of the younger women to the walls. Her brothers,
ten and twelve years old, stood guard with the men. All day and night
she had the men shouting orders loudly, and guns going on one side then

another, and she patrolled the fort calling at intervals, "All is well!"

As Madeleine stood guard she held a musket ready, and whenever she caught sight of a painted warrior she ordered a soldier to fire the cannon. The Iroquois believed that the fort was well defended, and so they hung around it for a week, firing occasionally, but not willing to storm the walls. The girl commander slept only in short naps by day, and never at night. At the end of the week, when the people in the fort were nearly exhausted, Madeleine heard a voice at the entrance. It was dark, but a thin moon shed a little light.

"Who goes there?" she called from the firing platform. Her breath almost choked her as she heard a man shout in French, "It is I, Lieutenant La Monnerie! I have brought forty men from Montreal to relieve the fort."

Madeleine told a soldier to stand guard at the gate, and she opened the door. Walking gravely up to the officer she saluted him, saying,

"Lieutenant, I surrender my command to you."

La Monnerie stared in astonishment at the little girl, then he returned the salute and said,

"Mademoiselle Verchères, I accept the command."

Madeleine de Verchères grew up to be the wife of Thomas Naudiere, and the mother of many children. Never again was she called on by circumstances to defend an outpost, but neither she, nor her fellow Canadians, ever forgot the week in which she held the fort against the fierce Iroquois with the skill and courage of a soldier.

WHEN THE English fur trading company entered Hudson Bay, guided by Radisson and Groseillers, a boy of fourteen came along. Henry Kelsey was keen for adventure and here he found plenty of it. Still in his teens he went out on journeys into the west from the English forts in the regions of the big bay, and he liked the Indians and they liked him.

To the Company of Adventurers Trading into Hudson Bay he was known as "that active lad, Henry Kelsey." He made journeys with Indian companions along unknown rivers, where muskeg, or moss, grew on barren rock and there was not enough wood to make a fire. He saw the strange musk ox of the north, and he also traveled to the south from Hudson Bay, into forests and onto plains, where he was probably the first white man to see the west's vast herds of buffalo.

From each long journey Kelsey returned to York Factory, the post at Hudson Bay. Here he reported to the factor and officers on Indian life, the furring trade and the unknown country. Kelsey kept a diary of his adventures. As he traveled among the different tribes he promoted peace among them, and persuaded them to bring their furs to the Hudson's Bay Company. During winter nights in the fort Kelsey, who was later made governor, spent his time writing a dictionary of Indian and Eskimo words for the company men who would go out fur trading. Kelsey was one of the men who enabled the Hudson's Bay Company to keep its hold on the fur trading of the north, in spite of the energy and skill of Frenchmen such as the Le Moyne brothers, leading expeditions that took outlying posts more than once.

While the English company was growing stronger in the north and west, the governors of French Canada continued to struggle with a rising illegal fur trade. Pelts were smuggled in great numbers into Montreal and Three Rivers, where the free ranging coureurs de bois made secret deals with certain ship captains. The most successful way that the government found to compete legally with the smuggling was the Montreal Fur Fair, which was held once each year, and which attracted Indians in large numbers.

For several days before the opening of the fair the Ottawa River was noisy and gay with as many as five hundred Indian-manned canoes swinging down it. The braves wore their brightest garments, feathers

and paint, and squaws and children laughed and chattered as canoes were beached. Camps were set up on river banks, and the Indians carried their loads of furs to the market in town. The governor came for the opening, to sit in a chair out of doors and to welcome the chiefs, who made long speeches.

The buying and selling lasted three days. As business was concluded Montreal citizens went indoors, put up their bars and closed their windows, for Indians and wild French woodsmen celebrated with brandy and ran through the streets, whooping, and fighting with knives and tomahawks. When the spree ended, the dead were buried, the wounded were taken care of by nuns in the hospital, and the sobered Indians and woodsmen disappeared upriver again. As the songs of French traders died out in the distance Montreal settled down once more to the quiet sound of church bells.

CHAPTER XV   THE FIRST SCIENTIST

TWO CITIZENS stood on a muddy street watching an Indian mount stone steps to a doorway. He carried a large woven basket from which the tops of reddish-green plants thrust outward. As the door closed behind the Indian the leather worker turned to his friend, a carpenter who was on his way to work at the shipbuilding plant.

"What can Père Sarrazin be doing, Jacques. Day after day I see Indians coming to his door with queer plants, and sometimes with dead animals. They do say that Michel Sarrazin, who is surgeon for the troops, has mighty strange ways. And what of that room of his, the one that nobody sees, but only hears about from his housekeeper?"

The carpenter shrugged, "Who knows? But, whatever it is, there is nothing evil about it. I heard only yesterday at the apothecary shop that in Paris the great doctors think well of our surgeon-major, and have made him a member of the Royal Academy of Sciences. I heard it from a gentleman returned from France by the same ship as Père Sarrazin himself."

Inside the largest room of the stone house Michel Sarrazin sat at a long table where the best light of the summer day fell on his microscope. He was unaware of his curious neighbors, walking away from his door. The table was piled high with dry brown plants of many kinds. Among them the skeleton of a beaver was carefully laid out on a mat. The room

was filled with books, plants, papers and even the carcases of animals. The scent was strong, but was unnoticed by the scientist. Sarrazin had been collecting and making studies ever since his arrival in the colony in 1685.

He heard a soft footstep, and turned around to see an Indian holding out a basket filled with reddish-green plants. Sarrazin's eyes brightened, as he stood up, thanked his friend and gave him a paper of sugar loaves and one of tobacco. Wooden boxes packed with wet moss stood about on the cluttered floor, and the scientist took the plants eagerly, yet with careful fingers. As he held the big oddly shaped things in his hands, he smiled. Here, indeed, was a wonderful specimen for his friend, the famous botanist, Tournefort, in Paris. Here was the insect-eating pitcher plant, a marvel to French scientists. Sarrazin's finger gently traced the pitcher shaped leaves and sharp hairs, the sticky passage to trap unwary insects, and the cavity where digestion took place.

Tomorrow the ship sailed for France. He was sending many new plants and animals to Europe, to add to the collection that he had already supplied—the blueberry, the sugar maple specimen, and now the pitcher plant. He had dissected and made microscopical records of the structure of the porcupine, the beaver, the seal and the muskrat.

"A fine collection," he murmured with satisfaction. "I have done well with this shipment." And he knew that his work was of exceptional value to the science of that day. The pitcher plant attracted much attention on its arrival across the ocean, and was named sarracenia, in honor of the first scientist of New France.

CHAPTER XVI

ON THE PLAINS OF ABRAHAM

IN THE last years of New France there were two men who will not be forgotten by Canadians: Francois Bigot, the last intendant, the worst man ever to hold authority, and the Marquis de Montcalm, a great soldier and an honorable man. Montcalm was sent to Canada to save the colony from the English and the Iroquois, but he could not hope to succeed with Bigot and the foolish governor, Vaudreuil, in charge.

While Montcalm, the military commander, struggled with his campaign plans in cold, bare quarters, eating the same poor rations of the citizens and the soldiers in these terrible winters, Bigot was stealing most of the funds sent out from France for the support of the colony. He lived in a large palace in Quebec, and spent money royally, as the dissolute king of France did across the water. His fine carriages and sleighs, his beautiful horses and grand living were all maintained at the expense of the people of Canada. When funds ran low Bigot signed playing cards and issued them as money.

The English, with William Pitt to run things, were expanding their seapower and Englishmen in the colonies of America were pushing out westward and northward. While New France remained small, English colonies grew rapidly. The Seven Years' War in Europe between France and England brought the French and Indian War to America. General Montcalm wrote back to France that this was a place where thieves grew rich and honest men went hungry.

In spite of a few successful campaigns Montcalm's troubles increased. Louisbourg, the strong stone fortress on Cape Breton Island, which had been lost in 1745 and then returned by treaty, was again taken by the British, and this time for good. One of the attackers was an officer to become famous in Canada, an Englishman, James Wolfe, fighting here his first campaign in America. General Montcalm knew that it was only a matter of time before Quebec itself would be attacked.

When the largest fighting fleet ever sent to America from England

sailed up the St. Lawrence, Montcalm watched with a desperate quiet. He intended to keep New France or die in the attempt. A hundred and forty ships anchored before the great rock in June of 1759. It was not an easy campaign for General Wolfe, for Quebec was a natural fortress in itself, and was defended by brave and determined men, both soldiers and citizens. All summer Wolfe tried to find a way of taking Quebec. He bombarded the city, and brought houses down in ruins, but could not take the fortress at the rock.

September arrived with its threat of a frozen river. Inside Quebec people set their pale faces and tightened their belts. They had no intention of giving up either, although they were living on dried horse meat. From time to time men from Montreal climbed a steep secret path to the top of the rock to bring supplies to the besieged at night.

Since this was the only spot where troops could get up the cliffs from the river, General Montcalm sent men to guard it. But the stupid governor ordered the troops back to Quebec. Wolfe heard of this path. One night, as wind whipped down cold from the north, a string of barges laden with five thousand English soldiers moved quietly upriver. When they were challenged the sentries were answered by a French deserter. Thinking that these men brought food to the starving city, the sentries let them pass.

By dawn the rock had been scaled, and British troops took up position for battle on the Plains of Abraham, where Louis Hèbert had cut his farm from the forest. Montcalm massed his troops for defense. On these grassy heights scarlet-coated English and kilted Scottish troops faced an army of white uniformed Frenchmen, blue-clad Canadian militiamen, coureurs de bois and Indians in buckskin, with their long-barreled rifles and steady eyes. Before the Canadian army rode General Montcalm, in full dress uniform, on his black horse.

The gallant French forces advanced, firing at the scarlet and tartan lines massed solidly before them. Again and again they were mowed down and hurled back by English forces. At last Montcalm himself was hit and badly wounded. As the Canadians retreated the general was held on his horse by two soldiers, who led him into the citadel of St. Louis to the surgeon. The fierce battle ended fifteen minutes after it began, and within a few hours Montcalm was dead.

On the Plains of Abraham General Wolfe, leading his well-trained and well-armed troops, was also wounded. He died there, in the field among the dead and injured—English, Scottish, French and Indian.

When General Townshend marched into the city the fleur-de-lis standard of France was brought to earth, and the flag of Britain snapped out on the autumn breeze. General Montcalm was buried in the walls of the Ursuline chapel, but Bigot, the evil man of the colony, and Vaudreuil, the weak and dishonest governor, escaped to Montreal and then to France.

Although Montreal managed to hold off the invaders for a year after the Battle of the Plains of Abraham, finally it too had to surrender. France, once the proud possessor of so much of the North American continent, had lost Canada to the English.

CHAPTER XVII   KING OF THE MOHAWKS

JOSEPH BRANT was the English name of a proud chieftain of the Mohawks. Like other members of the tribes of the Five Nations he hated the French and joined the English in the French and Indian War. As a child Brant had attracted the interest of an Englishman, who had sent him to be educated in a charity school for Indian boys in New England.

When the war for American Independence broke out Brant led the

Iroquois as allies of the English, and his warriors were responsible for some of the bloodiest massacres ever known in the Mohawk Valley. By the end of the war Brant was an officer in the British army, with a commission of colonel. After the British colonies became the United States, Joseph Brant was given an estate on the Grand River in Ontario.

The tall handsome Mohawk chieftain went to England and was presented at a royal audience to the king. As Chief Brant stepped forward in his most regal Indian attire, King George extended his hand to be kissed. Brant stood proudly, refusing to bend to kiss the hand of the monarch, saying:

"I am a king."

On another evening, while attending a state ball, Brant thought that he had been insulted by the Turkish ambassador. He sprang at the dignitary, tomahawk in hand, and it took some quick work on the part of his friends to prevent him from getting a Turkish scalp.

Yet, for all of his proud bearing and fierce spirit, Joseph Brant spent much of his time in Canada doing missionary work among his people. It was he who raised funds to build the Mohawk Chapel, the first Episcopal church for Indians in Canada. He also translated the Episcopal Prayer Book into the Mohawk language, and then did the same for the Gospel of St. Mark. The city of Brantford, Ontario, is named for him. The Mohawks under Brant were not the only people to move to Canada after the American War for Independence. Many English colonists who remained loyal to the British government carried their belongings north above the border and became Canadians. Most of them settled in Ontario and Nova Scotia.

CHAPTER XVIII   ACADIA

The Acadians in Nova Scotia had been under an easy English rule since 1713, though they had refused to swear allegiance to a Protestant king in England. The Norman farmers tended a pleasant fruitful land and went their way guided by their old customs and by their priests. Then, forty-two years later, when British were fighting French-Canadians, an Acadian priest, Abbé Le Loutre, joined the Indians to ambush and kill English soldiers. He even paid the Micmac tribe for English scalps, so harsh measures were taken by the rulers.

Without warning the Acadians were told to assemble at the shore,

and were placed on different ships and sent to various colonies, from Prince Edward Island in Canada to Georgia, and many made their way to New Orleans in Louisiana. Their houses and farms were destroyed, and the pathetic refugees wandered from place to place.

Parents and children were separated, and lovers were parted. Among these, according to legend, was a girl named Evangeline. She was about to be married to Gabriel, a neighboring farmer's son. She was taken on one ship to Philadelphia, and Gabriel on another to the Mississippi River. Their story, as Longfellow tells in his poem, describes the painful wandering of the girl in search of her lover, and of their meeting only when they were both old and Gabriel lay dying in a hospital.

Some of the Acadians finally made their way back to their homeland in Nova Scotia. Those who went to Louisiana became known as "Cajuns," and their descendants are still living among the bayous on the river.

CHAPTER XIX   ON UNKNOWN RIVERS

AT THE CLOSE of the eighteenth century the vast lands of the northwest were still unexplored by white men, except where fur traders had traveled along a few of the rivers. In 1789 a young Scotsman, Alexander Mackenzie, partner in the North West Company of Montreal, went scouting for furs. This company, recently formed of several smaller groups, was the only competitor of the powerful Hudson's Bay Company.

Mackenzie's thoughts were divided between furs and explorations. His immediate goal was trade but as so many before him had dreamed, so he did also of the fabulous Northwest Passage.

Four long canoes moved swiftly away from Fort Chipewyan, on western Lake Athabaska and into Great Slave Lake, where in early June ice had broken just enough for passage. Along the shores the canoes glided cautiously, and the men were forced to camp from time to time to wait until it melted. Toward the end of the month they entered the big river that now bears the name of the young Scotsman, who rode in the lead canoe. The Indian paddlers, led by one known as the English chief, grew more frightened as the great river spread out ahead of them. This stream collected water from other large rivers, to pour them northward into the Arctic Ocean. It was unknown country to these Indians

from farther south, yet they had heard stories of fierce cannibals who lived on its shores.

These were the Dogribs and the Hares, who turned out to be so terrified both of these men from the south, and of the warlike Eskimos of the north, who raided them from time to time, that they ran for the woods at sight of any strange canoe.

Mackenzie followed the river north to its mouth, and then turned back, disappointed, for he now knew that this way did not lead to the spices and silks, the rubies and gold of the Orient. But he was a bold and determined Scot. His second trip was made in one long but light canoe with ten men and a dog. They moved into the Peace River with its boiling rapids, where they almost drowned when the canoe capsized, and from the Peace they ascended the Parsnip. Then they crossed the Continental Divide to the wide Fraser River, making friends with the fierce Carrier Indians, who directed them toward the ocean.

After two months of incredible hardships the men reached the shores of the Pacific Ocean. Here Mackenzie, the first white man to penetrate.

the northern Rockies, wrote his name on a boulder in red paint mixed with bear's grease. Alexander Mackenzie returned to Scotland to spend his last years in his native land. In his misty highlands he could remember that he had not only left his name to the mighty river of the northwest, but that he had, with his explorations, extended Canada's horizon from ocean to ocean.

CHAPTER XX   WAR ON THE LAKES

TWO MEN looked sharply at each other as they shook hands in a log house at the western end of Lake Erie. It was midnight, and the light of two candles flickered on a rough table, where captured maps of the American commander, General Hull, lay spread out. This was August 14, 1812. Canada, an English colony, was at war with the young but vigorous United States. General Isaac Brock searched the eyes of the tall Shawnee chief, Tecumseh, and thought them proud, intelligent and sparked with vitality. Tecumseh looked at the blond English general and nodded his head. Then he turned to his Indian companions, saying, "This is a man!" These two were the best of their kind—Tecumseh the greatest of the eastern Indians and Brock an able officer and a brave man.

Tecumseh drew from his buckskin shirt a roll of elm bark and, bending over the table, he marked out with his scalping knife a map of the area around Fort Detroit. Brock decided on attack.

Next day the battle was short and was soon won by the Canadians. As the general and the chief rode forward together to enter the captured fort, Brock gave his belt and pistols to his Indian friend and Tecumseh presented his gaily colored sash to the general. This English commander had only a small number of troops to oppose the much larger, though badly prepared army of Americans attacking Canada. He knew that some powerful interests in the United States wanted to conquer and annex Canada, and he knew that he would get little help from England, too busy fighting Napoleon far away on land and sea. Tecumseh had brought Indians from the middle west to join the British, for they hated the Americans who were pushing them out of their old hunting grounds so rapidly.

The war between Canada and the United States was fought along the Great Lakes, the St. Lawrence River and the coasts. General Brock was its hero in Canada, although he did not live to see its end. While he was

at Fort George he received word that American troops had crossed the
Niagara River into Canada, and were already entrenched on the heights
at Queenston, defended only by a small detachment. As the general
galloped alone along the seven miles from the fort to the heights he
pushed his gray horse, Albert, as hard as possible. Brock knew that this
was a crucial time in Canadian history. If the Americans could invade
successfully here and split Canadian forces, the war might be lost. If
they could be forced back across the river time would be gained for
defense.

At Queenston Heights General Brock rallied his few troops and,
sword in hand, led them on foot up the hill to attack. As the tall scarlet-
coated commander reached the crest a bullet found its mark and he was
killed. When his men saw the body of their general lying on the ground
wearing the arrow decorated sash of Tecumseh, they stormed the hill
again and again. Each time they were forced back until reinforcements,
Canadians and Indians together, arrived. As they charged up the hill
yelling their dreaded war cries, the Americans turned and retreated back
across the river.

Canada gathered its forces, and the war continued around the lakes.
In the following year, not far from Queenston Heights, a backwoods
woman named Laura Secord went out at dawn to milk her cow. The
animal had strayed, and as she tracked it down she caught sight of two
American soldiers. They had not noticed her, and she heard them say
that American forces had succeeded in crossing the river and a surprise

attack was planned on Beaver Dams. She was living alone, for her husband was away somewhere with the Canadian army. Quietly Laura guided her cow past the sentries with a twig and into the forest. When she was out of sight she ran, stumbling through the bush, her dress torn to shreds by brambles. She waded through streams and made her way in and out of swamps for twenty miles to the Canadian camp. When she arrived she was almost too exhausted to gasp out the news.

Tecumseh, after the death of his friend Brock, had little confidence in other officers. He led his men in battles, but he grew despondent when Captain Perry, the American naval hero, was so successful on the lakes that he prevented supplies from reaching the Canadians, and Tecumseh's warriors were hungry. He told his braves that even if their allies retreated, he would not, for he would die in battle. Tecumseh felt that the battle on the Thames River would be his last stand, for he had had a dream that told him so.

As the Americans attacked on the banks of the river, Tecumseh fixed his eyes on Colonel Johnson, the enemy commander, and raised his silver tomahawk. As the American leader went down in death he raised his pistol and shot Tecumseh. After the American victory Tecumseh's warriors crept into the camp of the enemy and took away the body of their chief, to bury it secretly in the forest.

Peace negotiations that ended the war brought claims of success from both of these North American nations. Although the city of Washington had been partly burned by the British, victories had been won by the Americans also. The United States had become a stronger nation, and Canada, although still a British colony, was now aware of her own independent strength. She had not been conquered.

CHAPTER XXI   # THE LITTLE EMPEROR

THE VOYAGEURS, men of the long canoe and the bateaux, paddled for hours to the rhythm of their French songs. It was their muscles that for many years moved the freight of Canada down the rivers and across the lakes. These men, once hating the Hudson's Bay Company, were swept into it in 1821 when the North West Company merged with its rival. Now, from its headquarters in Montreal, the mighty company ruled half a continent, with its reputation for fairness strong among the Indians. It was run by an energetic little Scotsman who was a genius at organization and a remarkable leader.

Sir George Simpson insisted on fair dealing with factors, who were managers of the trading posts, voyageurs, and Indians. He cut down the rum and brandy trade that had ruined so many of the tribesmen. Simpson was known as the Little Emperor, and his arrival at a distant post was a big event.

On a crisp, chill day in autumn the sound of singing mingled with the shrill piping of a bagpipe came up the Columbia River to Fort Vancouver. Instantly the post snapped into activity. From the open gate with its enormous brass lock, set in a wooden wall twenty feet high, Indian squaws and their children ran, laughing and chattering, to the river bank. Guns boomed, flags whipped in the breeze, men in buckskin and Indian braves wrapped in blankets headed for the landing. The factor, tall, domineering old Dr. John McLoughlin, slapping his high beaver hat on his head, walked like a monarch to greet the only man who had more authority than he did in this wilderness. McLoughlin was called the White Headed Eagle, and his beaked-nose face and heavy body, dressed in knee breeches, fancy shirt and red cape, was held in awe by Indian and trapper. Before him marched his Scotch pipers.

Up to the landing swept a brigade of long canoes, manned by voyageurs and Indians. The brigade had halted around the bend to put on bright sashes, caps, beaded ornaments and feathers. The first canoe, bearing the painted insignia of the company, carried Sir George. Behind him, standing with feet braced carefully in front of the Indian paddlers, was the kilted piper, making his music skirl. In the following canoes voyageurs roared out their river song, "A la Claire Fontaine."

That evening the governor sat at dinner in the great hall of the fort, with his host and company officials of the post. Spread out before them was a feast of wild birds, buffalo tongues, venison, fish and many wilderness delicacies. Afterwards the Little Emperor got down to business and called for a strict accounting from his men. Simpson was tireless in his job. He loved a display, and knew that ceremony appealed to the Indians, but he could also travel the roughest trails by horseback, and in winter he went by dog sled or on snowshoes. He could sleep on the ground and eat pemmican, the Indian's sun-dried buffalo meat, ground up with berries. In 1825 George Simpson left with a party of ten men, on horseback, to go five hundred miles overland from Saskatchewan to the Red River. His journal tells of the trip:

"The last 24 hours I think have been the most uncomfortable I ever

passed. The water (in the Qu'Appelle River) was too deep to wade, and there was no wood to make a raft—several of our people could not swim and the bottom so soft there was the utmost danger of drowning. . . . I, however, being more at home in the water and anxious to save the lives of the poor horses, stripped and swam across with three others the whole of our little baggage; those people who could not swim holding on to the horses tails, and with the assistance of cords we hauled the poor animals out of the mud. In like manner we crossed the Assiniboine River, having occupied 5 hours . . . over the 2 rivers . . . naked in the mud and water exposed to the blood-thirsty assaults of myriads of musquetos, in short I believe there never was an unfortunate Governor in such a Woeful plight as that of the Northern Dept. of Ruperts Land this Day."

In Oregon families were rolling in, cutting trees and planting fields. In Canada, just to the north of them, the Hudson's Bay Company opposed settlers, for they ruined trapping and hunting. So here for years the Little Emperor ruled to the advantage of trader and Indian. He made the Hudson's Bay Company, from old McLoughlin's Fort Vancouver north to Rupert's Land, and on to the great bay itself the most powerful company of its kind ever known. Later, although the furring trade no longer flourished with the coming of settlement to western Canada, the company, changing its posts into general stores, stayed in the territory that it had done so much to develop.

CHAPTER XXII   PAPINEAU AND THE TINY CREATURE

IN THE VALLEY of the Richelieu River, between Quebec and Montreal, habitants gathering around a decorated pole in the village of St. Denis talked excitedly. A farmer from a distance stood beside his wagon asking, "Who is this Papineau? You say he is a grand seigneur, and a member of the Quebec Assembly? Then why does he talk beside that pole?" A knot of men and women turned to him. One said,

"This is the liberty pole. Papineau and the Sons of Liberty planted it. Why?—for freedom! Freedom from the English! Our stomachs are empty, no? Our crops are failing. Papineau says—"

A woman pointed at the tall man called Papineau, saying "See how handsome he is!"

Louis Papineau talked better, however, than he acted. The revolution

of 1837, led in Quebec by this tall man, and in Upper Canada, or
Ontario, by a small man named William Lyon Mackenzie, had no real
plan behind it. People listened because of their poverty and because of
their hatred of the local government. In Quebec province, although
there were some battles with troops, the uprising did not last long.
Armed soldiers easily scattered the habitant farmers, and their priests
thundered at them, for the Catholic church stood with civil authority in
spite of its dislike for the Protestant English. Papineau soon fled into the
United States.

In the town of York, which was later to become Toronto, Mackenzie
also poured out revolutionary speeches. He was known as the Tiny
Creature, and he ran a newspaper which continued to call for revolt
against the government, in the face of much opposition from the wealthier
citizens. When his enemies threw his printing type into Lake Ontario
Mackenzie sued them and was awarded damages with which to start his
newspaper again.

Mackenzie had absorbed the political ideas of the United States and
wanted Canada to become a republic. He kept in touch with Papineau,
and the two separate revolts began at the same time.

On a frozen night in December this queer-looking little man, wrapped
in a huge coat that scarcely allowed his whiskers to be seen, sat on a
white horse shouting to a confused crowd of farmers, many of whom
were armed only with sticks and pitchforks. They started a march on
York from the Montgomery Tavern outside town, and straggled down
Yonge Street behind the small figure on the big white horse. A few

shouldered ancient muskets, some carried pikes, and there were brave banners calling for "Liberty or Death!"

The governor at York rose from his warm bed, called out his troops, and waited for the rebels with gun in hand. As torches lighted the way frightened farmers approached the governor's forces drawn up on Gallows Hill. The governor shouted a request to talk things over. Furious at this turn of events Mackenzie tried to roar out a rejection, but his men were greatly relieved. They hesitated, and then refused to advance, already sorry that they had come out at all. The governor had food passed to the cold and hungry rebels, and at this sight Mackenzie was so wild that he flung himself from his horse, grasped a torch, ran to a house and set it on fire. His men, now scared of him instead of the governor, disappeared hurriedly up Yonge Street.

Nevertheless Mackenzie would not admit defeat, and he could be persuasive. Next day he talked some of the farmers into another advance, but at the first sound of firing they turned and ran again. Colonel Fitz-Gibbon, who had been an officer in Isaac Brock's army, led an attack on the Montgomery Tavern, where the remaining rebels were gathered. When they came out the governor ordered the tavern burned down. This time many arrests were made, but fiery little Mackenzie escaped across Lake Erie in a rowboat, disguised as a bewhiskered old woman. He set up his headquarters on a Canadian island near Niagara, and here made a plan that almost succeeded in bringing about war between Canada and the United States, for there were a few American hot-heads who still hoped to annex Canada. Fortunately London and Washington agreed to a settlement before much damage was done in some armed raids.

Eventually both Papineau and Mackenzie were allowed to return and Mackenzie was elected to Parliament. Later the grandson of Mackenzie, William Lyon Mackenzie King, became prime minister of a Canada that had, by that time, become an independent nation federated with Great Britain.

Although the revolts of 1837 failed, and in some aspects were absurd, they convinced the young Queen Victoria and her advisors that reforms were needed. Lord Durham was sent to Canada. He did not really understand the claims of the French there, and this made friction that lasted for years. However, in spite of language and religious differences, Durham did bring about a union between Quebec and Ontario, and both provinces were given equal representation in the Canadian Parliament.

CHAPTER XXIII

THE MIGHTY LOGGER

PAUL BUNYAN was the mightiest logger in all North America. They say that he was as tall as the highest pine tree, and as strong as Niagara Falls. Like the great waterfall, he is claimed by both Canada and the United States. Paul Bunyan could roll the biggest log ever cut, and the stories about him since the eighteen-thirties are the tallest tales ever told.

The real Paul Bunyan was boss of a lumber camp in Canada, a job that took a man who was outsize and tough. He was a French Canadian, and when the voice of Papineau was heard calling for revolt Paul stormed into battle in the village of St. Eustache. Behind him came loggers out of the big woods, swinging cant hooks and axes. But Paul was the giant of a man who scattered the Queen's troops with his roaring rage. Paul Bunyan got his reputation then, in the rebellion of 1837. Stories about his exploits spread from lumber camp to town and grew larger as they traveled.

In the autumn of every year from every town and village French lumberjacks made for the logging camps. In the deep snows of winter they cut and hauled, working from sunrise to sunset. At night, after a huge meal of pea soup and beans, salt pork and sourdough bread, they sat in the shanties and talked around the cambose. This was a fireplace built in the middle of the room. And early next morning they woke to the roar of cook's voice with his "Roll out or roll up!" meaning "Roll out of your bunk and get to work, or roll up your bedding and go."

Around the cambose a logger got out his fiddle and struck up a tune, and the bearded men sang the old songs made famous by the voyageurs in their long canoes. Then a logger said, "Did you ever hear how Paul danced and kicked so high that he marked the ceiling with the caulks in his boot soles?" And another—"Old Paul could carry eight hundred pounds on a portage." And then somebody was sure to tell the first story of Paul—the legend on which the tales are all based—the story of how Paul found his giant blue ox, Babe, in the winter of the blue snow, and

of how Paul, with the help of Babe, and of Johnny Inkslinger, his book-keeper, invented the lumber industry. Paul Bunyan was the Big Boss Man of the Woods!

After the great days of fur trapping, logging and lumbering became the most important work. The first big mill in the country was built at a bend of the Ottawa River, in Bytown, on the place later proclaimed by Queen Victoria as Ottawa, the capital city of Canada. The need to supply the lumber mills and to fill the holds of ships with timber for export kept loggers pushing ever deeper into the woods. On holidays shantymen amused themselves with dangerous birling contests, when two men twirled a floating log around with their feet, trying to hurl each other into the fast water. When loggers came to town for the first time in months they squandered their wages recklessly. Their French, Irish, Scotch and Scandinavian languages and tales have all had a part in making the Bunyan legends and keeping alive the memory of Paul, the giant strong man of the woods.

For many years squared timber was floated down the rivers for export to England for ship building, and to the United States. Older people can still remember the huge log rafts in the St. Lawrence, with their long sweeps, or oars, and their cabins where whole families lived for the voyage downriver. Now the tall white pines, many of them more than 200 feet high, that used to be cut for timber, are gone, but Northern Ontario is still important to the logging industry, and cutting of saw-logs and pulpwood for paper making makes Canada a world leader.

To preserve the forests Canada maintains the largest forest fire department in the world. Fire rangers are trained to keep a constant watch from steel towers rising above the tops of trees, to fly planes in fire-watching patrols, and to maintain fire-fighting headquarters in all wooded areas. They try to teach the settler that the tree is not his enemy, to be cut and burned recklessly, but in reality it is his best insurance for prosperity.

CHAPTER XXIV   KINGDOM OF THE WEST

THE PEOPLE called Métis were a different kind—different from the Indians who were their ancestors, and different also from the French and Scotch who had intermarried among the tribes of the Western prairies and produced these people of the Red River country. They were called *bois brulé*, or the color of burnt wood, and they were hunters of buffalo and trappers of furs. The Métis, which means mixed blood, people had lived in this grassy land between the Great Lakes and the Rockies for a hundred years.

Of all of the wild brown men of the Métis their leader, Louis Riel, was the strangest. He was an educated man, who had studied for the priesthood in Montreal. Louis Riel was obsessed with a dream of becoming the undisputed ruler of a great western empire. He was part French, part Indian, and was only twenty-four when he became the recognized leader of the people of the plains, whose independent little nation was called Assiniboia. Riel's own people, like the Indians, did not want to lose their hunting grounds and homes. French trappers and traders were Catholics and they resented the importation of Scottish highlanders who were coming in as part of a farming settlement scheme devised by Lord

Selkirk, with the approval of the government.

When surveyors arrived from eastern Canada, in October, 1869, to prepare Manitoba to become a Canadian province, Riel led fifteen Métis to warn them off. These wild brown hunters would yield to no Canadian from the east.

They were independent of all authority in the matter of furs too. Métis lived on both sides of the border and paid no attention to Canada or the United States. The Hudson's Bay Company had never been able to stop the Métis men from smuggling pelts across the American border to markets of their own. On a day in November of that year, by pre-arranged plan, the Métis below the border seized army officers sent out by Prime Minister Macdonald to take charge, and Louis Riel led a band of armed hunters to the Hudson's Bay Post of Fort Garry.

Without firing a shot the bois brulé took the fort. The old Hudson's Bay governor could do nothing. He lay dying in his bed and when he saw this young man, vigorous and wild-eyed, stride into his room, he said nothing. Riel stood before him, feeling that his dream was taking shape, and that he was truly a king in a captured stronghold. Setting up head-quarters, he strode about the fort dressed in a black frock-coated suit and a white ruffled shirt, with Indian moccasins on his feet. He had many of the qualities of a leader of men, but his mind was unstable.

Influential men in America sent an agent to try to persuade Riel to declare Assiniboia a part of the United States. But Riel, who disliked Canadian Protestants, still swore allegiance to the British crown. In Ottawa Macdonald and Parliament were angry, yet they could not decide what to do about Riel. A vast land of swamps, forests, lakes and rivers, with rapids and long hard portages lay between the government and its western territories.

Then Louis Riel had a young Irishman named Thomas Scott shot for taking part in a raid on Riel's headquarters. News of this so infuriated the Canadian Parliament that its hot demands for military action could not be ignored. Macdonald sent Colonel Wolseley with twelve hundred troops on one of the longest, toughest marches ever made on the American continent. The men took an old Indian trail north around Lake Superior, waded swamps, braved clouds of mosquitoes, and cut their way through to the west. When Louis Riel heard that the troops had arrived he lost his nerve and fled south across the border. Riel remained a hero to his people, but his unstable mind began to give way to spells of insanity.

CHAPTER XXV   BUFFALO HUNT

MÉTIS PEOPLE, like the Indians of the plains and prairies, lived on the buffalo. Each June they had a great hunt, in which men, women and children followed the enormous herds.

Southward down a long trail in Assiniboia wound a long line of more than a thousand Métis hunters, with their women and children, ponies, oxen and dogs. The men were handsome and strong. They wore buckskin embroidered with beads, the famous woven "Assomption" sashes so popular with Frenchmen and Indians, and black felt hats with beaded bands. The women, who were often beautiful, had black dresses and embroidered aprons and shawls, and everyone wore high moccasins.

The carts and horses moved toward Pembina in a vast cloud of dust. Red River carts, used for many years on these prairies, had crude wooden wheels bound with rawhide. They could transport quantities of heavy goods, but the screeching of the wheels as they turned on unpeeled wooden axles made a sound that no one but a Métis could endure.

At Pembina they were joined by more Métis, some Scotch-Indian, some French-Indian, as well as others from Dakota. Leaders of different groups met, captains were selected and rules agreed on for travel and for protection. Early next morning the wagons and carts rolled, wheels screeching, horses snorting, riders shouting, women and children singing in French, English and in the Cree Indian language.

Day after day the Métis moved, searching for a buffalo herd, and at night encamped under the summer stars. Scouts brought word that buffalo herds were near, and the camp moved into instant, orderly action. Priests came forward to bless the kneeling hunters, who then mounted their horses and lined up behind the elected chief. As his horse moved off the chief waved his arm and shouted, "Haw! Haw!"

When the buffalo heard approaching horses they turned and ran in a terrified stampede with the four hundred Métis hunters in wild pursuit. Dust rose into the sky, and the sound of hoofs was a thundering roar. Each man killed as many buffaloes as he could run down, firing, reloading and racing on. Many of the hunters dropped identifying pieces of cloth to claim their kill later on. Danger ran with them, for there were always men and horses injured and sometimes killed in a great hunt. It did not last long, and when the shooting was over the butchering took place swiftly, with the women coming in to help, bringing the carts to carry meat back to camp.

The meat was cut in strips and hung on poles to dry in the hot sun. After several days some of the dried meat was pounded into a powder and mixed with wild berries to make pemmican, and then packed tightly into buckskin bags. This concentrated food was the mainstay of Indian, Métis, hunter, trapper and Hudson's Bay man. From it a nourishing stew could be made, and it was eaten raw when necessary. From some hunts the Métis brought home as much as a million pounds of buffalo meat.

The buffalo skins were carried back to the Red River settlements and farms of Assiniboia, and traded to the Hudson's Bay Company. The Métis loved their freedom as did their Indian cousins. They spent little time on their narrow strips of grazing land and small farms along the rivers. Like the adventurous Frenchman they were brave and joyous, and like the Indian they would not give up their hunting lands easily.

Into the green valley of the Red River moved Scotch and English farmers to take over land held so long by the wandering Métis. Settlements were coming, and old Fort Garry, headquarters for hunters, trappers, and Indians of the Canadian west, was becoming the little town of Winnipeg, in the province of Manitoba.

CHAPTER XXVI   MEN OF THE MOUNTED

AT THE END of track, in the small town of Fargo, North Dakota, everybody gathered to watch the train arrive. The little puffing engine and cars were something still new to this western prairie, and the group of three hundred tired, dusty men in ordinary dress who stepped out onto the wooden platform thought Fargo strange enough. They were Canadians, from Quebec, and sent west by Prime Minister Macdonald and the Canadian Parliament of a nation now unified under confederation. As yet Canada was not even sure that the northwestern lands really belonged to it. In this year of 1874, it was easier to reach western Canada through the United States, with its new railroads fanning out westward, than through Canada itself.

Next day people in the dusty street blinked at the troopers. Led by Assistant Commmissioner Macleod they were mounted and ready to ride in red coats, blue breeches, cavalry hats and pistol belts. An old cowhand scratched his chin.

"They do say them fellows are the Canadian Northwest Mounted Police. One of 'em told me they are going to round up them whiskey traders that get the Indian's buffalo robes in trade for fire water." He laughed and slapped his leg. "Going right up to Fort Whoop-Up and catch them wild whiskey men and crazy drunk Indians? Its good-by for you, boys, when you try it." The other bystanders agreed with him.

The Mounties were few in numbers, but they were determined. They had sworn to "Uphold the Right," as their motto declared. As they rode north they had no idea of the troubles that lay ahead, but they meant to establish law and order. Down on the American plains United States cavalry fought the tribes in fierce and bloody battles, yet this first troop of Mounties, because they were so few, did not alarm the Indians.

When Colonel Macleod had set up his headquarters on Canadian territory, he sent his men out, two by two, to bring in the known criminals and the drunks. They also set out to help those who needed help. The brutal whiskey traders, who deliberately turned friendly Indians into drunken fiends, lived in Fort Whoop-Up, behind a log palisade guarded by cannon and rifles, and swore they would never be taken. The Mounted Police brought in a few whiskey traders, singly or by twos, taking them to Fort Macleod for trial. The bravado of the others weakened. In the end the colonel, who had thought that his men would have to take Fort Whoop-Up by armed assault, went in without firing a shot. People began to understand that the Mounted Police were not soldiers sent out to fight, but were peace officers, enforcing order and justice.

After the frightful massacre of Custer and his men at the Little Big Horn River, Sitting Bull and his tribe of Sioux crossed the border to live in Canada. Macleod expected serious trouble. Yet the chief looked long at this man in the scarlet coat, surrendered his four thousand armed braves and promised to live in peace. The Indian wars that swept across the American plains in these years did not extend above the northern border, for the tribes liked and respected the Northwest Mounted Police.

Then Louis Riel came back. The Métis had moved westward to the Saskatchewan River, away from Red River settlers, and once more they saw surveyors coming to divide their grazing grounds into farms, as the Canadian Pacific Railroad pushed westward. Riel had been living in Montana with his wife and two children, and had been teaching in a country school, although his mind was confused, and he believed himself to be a prophet. Again the Métis and Indians took up arms. In March, 1885, Riel and Dumont, the leader of the rebellion, struck at Duck Lake, killing twelve Mounted Police. Terrified settlers fled into small unfortified Fort Pitt, which was not even protected by a log stockade after the tiny settlement of Frog Lake had been almost wiped out by the

Crees. The situation was desperate for all of those within the fort as several hundred Métis and Cree Indians gathered ominously in the snowy forest across the river.

When the Crees under Chief Big Bear surrounded the cluster of buildings the commander, red-headed Inspector Francis Dickens, son of the famous English novelist, Charles Dickens, sat listening to the excited settlers. His hand drummed nervously on the table as he replied to their questions,

"A message has come in from Big Bear. He says that if you settlers give yourselves up he gives his word that none of you will be harmed. What do you want to do? We can't hold out long. There are just twenty-one policemen here."

An old man spoke slowly, "We will give ourselves up at dawn, if you Mounties will make a try for help." It was almost daylight, and the scow that the policemen would use was ready if needed. The inspector nodded grimly, "Very well. We will try to reach the fort at Battleford and bring help to you."

As the edges of the forest began to lighten under a gray sky the little group of settlers, made up of twenty-eight men, women and children, walked slowly toward the trees. As the Métis and Indians perceived them Dickens and his men pulled the scow, already loaded with ammunition and food, to the river and leaped into it. The crudely built boat swung crazily against cakes of ice as they pushed off. Shots spattered the water and the scow, but the men were too busy trying to stay afloat in the swift current to return fire. Drenched by water spilling over the sides, their clothing froze solidly until a wounded trooper looked like a block of ice. They had to bail frantically as the scow swung downriver.

After six days the Mounties reached Battleford, where they were taken more dead than alive into the fort, itself besieged by Indians and Métis. This post was protected by a log stockade, and although shots rang out from the woods as they were carried in the open gates, the Northwest Mounted Police band began to play. Big Bear kept his word, and the settler prisoners were not harmed by his Crees. They were later released, the Indians and Métis were defeated, and Louis Riel, with Dumont and his men, were once more subdued. Riel was captured and taken to a town called Pile o' Bones, later named Regina, where he was hanged as a traitor to Canada. With the death of Riel the independent nation of the Métis ended.

The men in scarlet coats spread out into all of the wild lands of the

northern Canadian west. They act as federal police in all of Canada, and as provincial police in all but Ontario and Quebec. They have traveled on horses, by dog sled, on snow shoes and on foot—and, more recently, in cars, airplanes and on motorcycles too. They still guard the far-flung reaches of lonely country, and they are known as the greatest police force in the world.

CHAPTER XXVII

BUSH PIONEERS

THERE STOOD vast Canadian forests, with tall pines, spruce, birch and maple so thick that the sun could scarcely penetrate the branches! Under the French, farms were carved out only along the St. Lawrence and in the Maritime Provinces. Men from England, Scotland and Ireland, as well as young French Canadians, became pioneers as they had to push farther into the wilderness with their wives and children, and the sound of axe and saw was heard in remote clearings.

Land was offered free by the Crown to officers who were veterans of the wars with Napoleon. Their wives, some of whom were well educated and used to comforts, toiled in log cabins with cooking pots over open fires, and made soap in kettles outside. Often on a hand-hewn puncheon floor a few pieces of fine polished furniture stood bravely, while behind the door hung the gold braided coat of an army or navy captain. It took courage to handle an axe and cut a pile of cordwood larger than the cabin itself for use during the long ice-bound winter. At best "corduroy" roads replaced trails to little towns, where the only gathering place was a church or a country store.

These pioneers lived in their tiny clearings, battling swarms of mosquitoes, grubbing stumps and sowing seeds in small fields. Often they trudged miles for sacks of flour and beans to be carried home on bent backs. Some gave up and returned across the sea. Those who stayed helped each other. An old sea captain might get into a black rage with his neighbor, an army man who was "fit for nothing better than riding a horse in front of his regiment." Yet when there was a barn raising or a turkey shoot they all came from miles around, and then celebrated the finished job with a dance that made the new rafters shake. The former officers learned to look with great respect at a farm job well done by a backwoods neighbor who had no schooling or city manners.

From these people in their bush clearings came stories that somehow spread, and that always drew a laugh no matter how often they were told. They made their own mistakes and troubles into tales, and sometimes songs, around the big fireplace.

"Did you ever hear tell of Ned and Jemima? Well—it goes like this— there was a young fellow over Lake Simcoe way. He lived on a farm with his mother and a pretty girl cousin. Now Ned was sweet on his cousin, Jemima, but too shy to say so.

"One July day, when it was so hot the sun was like to make the top of your head feel like a scorched slab of bacon, Ned took his scythe and went out to a beaver meadow to cut wild hay for the cows. So Ned, getting hotter as he worked, pulled off his britches to cool his legs. There he was, cutting away in his long-tailed shirt, boots and straw hat, when he felt a swish and heard a rattling sound.

"Ned leaped about six feet straight up, and came down running. He made for the cabin, dropping his scythe as he went, yelling, 'Snakes, varmints! Help!' "

"His mother ran out of the door and flapped her apron up and down at the terrible sight. Jemima came a-running too, and she didn't just stand there gawking. Around and around the cabin Ned was sprinting, with a bush rattlesnake fastened to his shirt and swinging out behind

like the tail of a race horse. The brave girl dashed into the cabin, grabbed the sheep shears, and on the next go-round neatly clipped off snake and shirt-tail together. Ned, with his mouth still open for a yell, stopped short, looked at the girl, and said, loud and clear,

" ' Let's get hitched, Jemima.'

" 'All right, Ned,' she said, 'but scotch that snake first, before he comes inside and sets up house-keeping.' "

CHAPTER XXVIII   ON TO THE PACIFIC!

IT TAKES many people, of many kinds, to make a nation, and sometimes they do it by design, and sometimes by accident. There were three men who played big parts in creating western Canada. Strangely enough, although one was a Scotchman, the other two were Americans.

A Scotsman named Duncan Fife, farming near Peterborough, Ontario, looked despondently at his unripened wheat crop, lost to an early frost. He asked a friend who was going to Europe to find him seeds that would ripen early. The friend forgot his promise until the day he was ready to return, and then, seeing a grain ship docked nearby, he begged a handful of wheat for Fife. Out of this little mound the three stalks that sprouted ripened ten days before frost. So it was, quite by chance, that wheat first flourished both in Ontario and in the rich black soil of the prairies, and Canadians came by the hundreds to grow it there.

The other two men who were to overcome the land and water obstacles to western expansion were Harvey and Van Horne. At Sault Ste. Marie, Charles Harvey built the first huge locks, to take ships sailing from eastern lake ports up into Lake Superior. This was the gateway to the West where in 1787, on the Canadian side, voyageurs had first dug a tiny canal to take their canoes and bateaux around the big rapids of the St. Mary's River, thus avoiding the long portage. The need became great when iron ore was found on Lake Superior shores and such cargoes could no longer be handled by the old method of hauling around the rapids in wagons. In 1855 Harvey watched with eager eyes as the first ship, the *Illinois*, passed through the locks and into the lake beyond.

The word *sault* means rapids, and on either side of them two towns grew. They had the same name, Sault Ste. Marie, although one was in Michigan and the other in Ontario. Now the great locks, with several added over the years, have a larger volume of ship traffic than the

Panama and the Suez canals combined.

William Van Horne was a great American engineer who declared that nothing could stop him from building a railroad to the Pacific. Trying to get into the West ahead of him was James Hill, a Canadian, already constructing the Great Northern Railroad in the United States, and pushing branch lines up into Canadian country. Huge, stout Van Horne pulled on his short black beard as he roared out that it would take more than Hill, hostile Indians, granite cliffs and swampy muskeg to stop him from laying track. His men started from both east and west at the same time, planning to meet in the Rockies.

As the shining rails moved forward Van Horne was beset with troubles. He could not get enough support from Parliament, because few of the men there realized the importance of the transcontinental railroad. Old Prime Minister Macdonald understood it, and he used every means in his power to keep money moving to Van Horne. His head was bowed with schemes to get help for the railroad as he walked the Ottawa streets in his black clothes, wearing the bright sash of the hunter and Indian, with a shawl clutched about his chilly shoulders.

In 1884 when war with the Métis and Indians broke out a second time troops had to be moved there quickly. The railroad was building, but nobody thought that it could carry soldiers west in time. For about 250 miles along the northern shore of Lake Superior tracks had not yet been

laid. Van Horne declared in his booming voice,

"I'll get troops there for sure in eleven days!"

He laid tracks on ice, through bogs and on soft muskeg in the melting snows of spring, where they sometimes sank from sight. He put in fill dirt, laid ties and rails and shoved along flat cars loaded with soldiers. When tracks could not be laid the men were hauled over solid ice on sleighs.

The five thousand soldiers arrived in nine days, the rebellion ended, and the support of Parliament for finishing the road was assured. In the first year Van Horne laid five hundred miles of track, and in the second eight hundred. On November 7, 1885, the last spike was pounded in by Donald Smith, Lord Strathcona, the financier who, with Lord Mountstephen had backed the difficult project. Lord Strathcona said, "This spike is not silver or gold, but it is as good a spike as you can find between Montreal and Vancouver and no better."

As yet Canada had very few settlements in the West, but nobody had any doubt now that this vast land was hers, and that she was a nation, from ocean to ocean.

CHAPTER XXIX · GOLD ON THE YUKON

There are strange things done in the midnight sun
By the men who moil for gold;
The Arctic trails have their secret tales
That would make your blood run cold;
The Northern Lights have seen queer sights
But the queerest they ever did see
Was that night on the marge of Lake Lebarge
I cremated Sam McGee.

ROBERT W. SERVICE, who wrote this and other ballads of the "sourdough," brought laughter and wonder to people all over the world. The wild and astonishing days of the Klondike gold rush started in 1896 when a man named Carmack found the first nuggets on Bonanzo Creek. At that time Service was a bank clerk in the rip-roaring town of Dawson, near the Arctic Circle. During his eight years there thousands of men, and some women, swarmed into Canadian Northwest Territory and Alaska, hunting gold. They came in light clothing with little food to a land where snow piled seventy feet deep on top of Chilkoot Pass. Real tales of the "sourdoughs" were almost as fantastic as the story of Sam McGee. According to Service, McGee was from Tennessee, and he minded no hardship on earth except the brutal cold. On the eve of his death he got a promise from his friend not to put him into an icy grave but to cremate him. Looking into the open door of the roaring furnace, the friend saw Sam grinning with joy and heard him call out, "Since I left Plumtree, down in Tennessee, it's the first time I've been warm."

In all of that vast land of ice and snow, where frozen peaks seem to touch the midnight sun, there lived only a few sparse tribes of wandering Indians and Eskimos. Then overnight everything changed. Every available ship, some no more than little floating tubs, sailed north, jammed with gold-hungry men.

Many of the tenderfeet, known as "chechakos," struggled up Chilkoot Pass and then tried to get downriver to the gold fields. For the protection of the prospectors a small troop of Mounted Police were stationed at the pass. They stopped the straggling hoards of bearded gold prospectors as they slogged their way through the pass, and turned them back if they had no food and money. Those who had money rented any boat available to float down the Yukon River. If they had none they walked a five-mile portage around the rapids. One of the boat pilots was a man later to be famous for *The Call of the Wild* and other novels about the far north. He was Jack London, an American, then twenty-one years old.

Dawson was the central town, filled with a brawling mob of prospectors, gamblers and crooks. The Mounties had a job that seemed impossible, but they handled it. Across the border in Alaska there was no law. The most famous desperado of the gold rush, known as Soapy Smith, retreated there when on the run. Within three or four years the Klondike was bursting with a population of thirty-thousand people, and then, as richer claims gave out, it dropped to a few thousand. Bigger mines were opened, to be worked with machinery, and the wild days of Robert W. Service were over. Missionaries set up little churches for Indians, Eskimos and remaining "sourdoughs."

These tiny towns, frozen in for seven months of the year, were only pinpoints in the desolate wastes of the Canadian north. Each spring everyone made bets on the date of the break-up of the ice, and gathered on the banks of the river at Dawson and other towns to see the end

of winter. They heard great chunks of ice cracking and pounding and watched the river move as if in a convulsion.

Yet even when the big gold rush was over every spring found many men with picks, shovels and pans, lined up in stores for grubstakes. They could not wait to start out for the cold rivers, the unknown mountains, and the claims that they hoped would make them millionaires.

CHAPTER XXX   PEOPLE OF THE SNOWS

UP IN THE Northwest Territory, where the sun shines near the Arctic Circle for half a year, and then disappears for the other half, two Eskimo boys went out to spear fish. Snow still lay deep, although it was early spring. They did not notice how the sky had darkened and the wind was blowing. Too-Too, the older boy, felt something wet falling on his face. He grasped Ootah by his mittened hand. The two stood and looked into a sudden blizzard raging around them. They could scarcely see each other.

Too-Too pulled his little brother's seal skin mittens off and made him sit down on them. He told Ootah to draw his arms inside his outer coat sleeves and fold them on his chest. Too-Too did the same, and they leaned forward with their elbows on their knees. Sitting this way the snow piled up around them, but they did not get very cold. They knew it was important not to lie down. After several hours the blizzard stopped

and the boys struggled back through the soft snow to their igloo. Their mother had not been worried, for all Eskimos know how to live safely in sub-zero weather, but she did scold them for not putting up a small snow shelter before the blinding blizzard struck hard.

Too-Too and Ootah were coast Eskimos. Their father often took them fishing and seal hunting. On warm summer days they went with their mother and little sister, who rode on her mother's back, to gather wild blueberries. Berries tasted good to them, but not as good as lumps of fat or spoonfuls of warm grease.

Eskimos move about a good deal, building their shelters wherever they are. They live in different tribes, as Indians do. In summer they make huts of sod and bark or tents of skins. In winter they build igloos of blocks of snow. Their homeland extends from northern Labrador to the shores of the Northwest Territory, down as far as Manitoba and across all northern Canada.

Inland in the far northern wilds west of Hudson Bay, where the tundra, or vast treeless plain, is frozen below the surface even in summer, the Caribou Eskimos live in wandering family groups. They are the people who follow the herds, dwelling among lakes in summer, spearing fish and shooting birds with crude bows made from caribou antlers and sinews. Several times through the year the herds of caribou move across the tundra in great migrations. And then, if it is winter, the Eskimos hunt them on dog sleds, with their women and children following to skin and cut up the meat. In summer they chase them on foot, and when the

caribou swim the tundra lakes the Eskimos paddle after them in light boats called kayaks.

Eskimos are not of the same race as the Indians, and are thought to have come across from Asia by way of Bering Strait at a later period than the first Indians did. They have had less contact with the white peoples than the Indians have had. Until a few years ago they lived just as their ancestors had for several thousands of years. Now this is changing. The vast northern wastes of frozen Canada have been invaded by men who are installing radios, radar, airplane bases and weather stations. Doctors fly in to establish better health centers to help the Eskimos, and supply posts are providing the primitive wandering "little people," as they are called, with food that is new to them. Churches have missions in these areas. In the million square miles of northwestern Canada there live only about sixteen thousand Eskimos, Indians and whites. Changes that are taking place in the northern territories are so rapid that the government in Ottawa knows that the nomadic peoples of the north will soon have to become settled in a kind of life that provides regular work.

This frozen land, so long unknown, is now the last frontier and the United States and Canada are building a chain of defense radar bases there called Operation Dew-Line. Eskimos are learning new ways from the newcomers—and the newcomers are also learning from the Eskimos how to live comfortably with snow and ice. Expert mechanics from Canada and the United States learn to their surprise that Eskimos are not only carvers of beautiful soapstone and ivory ornamental pieces, but that they possess great natural mechanical skills.

CHAPTER XXXI   THE UNSEEN

FOR THE Indians water, forest and sky were peopled by spirits. Some were good, as was Manitou the Great Spirit; some were evil, and some prankish and funny. Beloved of the Ojibway was Pawpawkeewis, the wanderer, who played jokes on them, scattering their camp fires, throwing leaves into the cooking pots and tripping up children. The strangest of all was the evil Wendigo.

The forest was good to the Indian, giving him meat for food, skins for clothing and birchbark for his fleet canoe and to cover his lodge. Yet the forest was fierce and relentless too, and if it was friendly it was also hostile to man. As white men came to know the Indian and the forest

they too began to believe in the Wendigo. There are strange tales told of its power. A solitary trapper, sleeping by his camp fire, wakes with a feeling of dread. He lies there, tense, listening. A bear may be prowling or a timber wolf may be crouched in the black fringe of forest, waiting. He knows that no bear or wolf will attack him unless he makes the first hostile move. It is something compelling, something mysterious as the darkness. A rank odor makes his nostrils quiver. He hears a small sound, like a little lost child crying, far away among the trees. He tries to stay by the safety of the dying fire, knowing that no real child cries. Then he stumbles to his feet, and flings himself into the darkness, running faster and faster.

Some would call it bush fever, or madness caused by loneliness. Two Indian hunters, finding his lifeless body, look at each other in fear. "It was the Wendigo," they say.

French Canadians have their legends too, and some are tragic and some are amusing. The habitants fear the devil, and yet they rather like him, for their stories are often about a contest between a man and the devil, and quite often the man will win. Pierre and Jacques, in the lumber camp shanty, will both laugh and cross themselves at the same time, as they tell tales of outwitting the devil. Yet they do not laugh at the dreaded werewolf, the *loup-garou*—a man turned into a wolf and doomed to wander the snows at night looking for someone to kill.

There is the story of the phantom canoe, paddled by the ghosts of voyageurs, singing their old songs as they sweep wildly across the skies in a snowstorm. The man who joins the ride of the phantom canoe, on New Year's Eve, to dance and sing all night at such a party as was never seen on earth, disappears into the skies with the ghosts when a cock crows at midnight. Or so they say! And there is the tale of the reckless Bastien who danced with the northern lights.

Once upon a time there was this fellow, Bastien, who played his fiddle until the shanty bullies kicked their boots as high as their heads, roaring with joy. *"A qui dansera le mieux"* he sang, and then he shouted up at the night sky, where the great bands of colored lights zigzagged back and forth. "Hoh!" cried Bastien, "I will fiddle for the lights, the marionettes, to dance in the midnight sky!"

Faster he fiddled, as he danced and played. The bullies fell on their faces on the ground, afraid to look, but Bastien played and sang, and danced. The lights moved, back and forth, up and down. Bastien played and sang and danced so fast that his feet left the earth and his dazzled eyes could not leave the marionettes, the northern lights, as they swirled and moved. At last the shantymen raised their heads to look. Away in the endless sky the marionettes were growing pale, as they moved toward the horizon. Bastien had gone with them. From a long way off they seemed to hear his voice—*"A qui dansera"*—and the sound of his fiddle. They never saw him again, but on a chilly night, as they watched the dance in the sky they would say, "Listen! It is Bastien. Hear him singing, *'A qui dansera le mieux'*?"

CHAPTER XXXII   THE FACE OF A NATION

At first Quebec alone was Canada. Then, with the coming of the people of the British Isles there were two Canadas—French-speaking Lower Canada and English-speaking Upper Canada, each colony with its own local government. After the Papineau and Mackenzie rebellions, the Act of Union, in 1840, joined the two.

In 1867 came Confederation when two maritime colonies, Nova Scotia and New Brunswick, entered the union and the Dominion of

Canada was born. A few years later Manitoba as well as little Prince Edward Island on the Atlantic coast and big British Columbia on the Pacific joined to make a nation, from sea to sea. The entrance of the prairie provinces of Alberta and Saskatchewan in 1905 brought the number to nine. In 1948 Newfoundland, including Labrador, made the tenth province. There are two territories, the Northwest and the Yukon. The government is built on the British plan of prime minister and cabinet from the majority party in Parliament, and Canada is now an independent nation within the British Commonwealth.

For more than a century Canadians, always adventurous, traveled long distances by canoe, bateau and York boat along the countless waterways of the north. Over rough roads horses, carts, stage coaches and covered wagons carried settlers ever farther from the cities. Yet the dense forests, difficult swamps and muskeg made distant settlement hard, and it took the railroads, pushing steel rails relentlessly forward, to populate the West with farms, cattle ranches and towns.

With the age of the automobile, truck and bulldozer, good roads reached out into wilderness. More settlers came from Europe, the United States and the British Isles. Now airplanes weave a network of travel from the Great Lakes and fishing regions of the coasts, both east and west, to the vast north. Planes carry sportsmen to lakes unapproachable by roads, and "bush pilots" ferry by air everything from mail to machinery. Commercial airlines link cities and provinces and carry travelers to all the world.

In the early days Canadians made their land important to Europe by trapping furs. Then farming spread over the wide acres of fertile soil where forest had been, and when the herds of buffalo had been killed, wheat fields took the place of buffalo grass on the prairies. Since the days of the first explorers, Europe's fishermen have caught cod and herring in the Atlantic off the coasts of Canada. In the rivers of British Columbia silver salmon are taken.

Oil production on the prairies of Alberta and Saskatchewan has changed western Canada with fantastic speed. Fifty years ago energetic pioneers from many countries came into the Northwest Territories to carve out farms. Now Canada's richest oil field, the Pembina, and others almost as productive, pipe oil to the eastern provinces, and many western farms are industrial centers, villages are towns, towns are humming cities.

Canada's great rocky base also produces minerals in Ontario and

Labrador. As early as 1770 Jesuit missionaries mined copper on the north shore of Lake Superior. Here and there iron smelters were built, and in 1846 silver was discovered at Thunder Bay. As the railroad was pushing through Ontario, a blacksmith noticed that copper showed in the rocks being blasted. Now Sudbury, with nearby Coppercliff, is one of the world's largest mining areas for copper, nickel and platinum.

Up in the bush country of northern Ontario another blacksmith, Fred LeRose, was walking along swinging his hammer in his hand. Seeing a flash of red fox fur he threw the hammer. Missing the fox it struck a mossy rock, and as he picked up his tool, LeRose saw that the rock had gray streaks in it. This was a vein of silver. The town of Cobalt soon sprang up as prospectors rushed in to make another wild and lawless frontier. Gold was also found by an Indian at Porcupine, and another stampede began.

With the development of great hydroelectric plants on the powerful streams where once voyageurs and Indians paddled, Canada is rising rapidly as an industrial nation. A pilot atomic power station is being built at Chalk River, and once again prospectors are coming into new

sites to stake claims and make sleepy little backwoods villages into boom towns. Now the rush is not for silver or gold, and prospectors do not carry pans for washing out gravel. Geiger counters in hand, they search for uranium and hope for a quick fortune as the old "sourdoughs" did in the Klondike. Uranium finds have been made before, but the new one now booming near Blind River, Ontario, is probably the richest in the world.

CHAPTER XXXIII　　　　　　　　　# THEY GIVE US CANADA

A BIT of chip tossing on rolling sea waves is not more alone than a solitary man plodding slowly, steadily, on a rough road through the Canadian bush. The young fellow whose muddy boots solidly yet wearily hit the road, which was scarcely more than a trail, carried on his back a knapsack holding his few belongings—extra wool socks, some underwear patched by kindly Madame Bédard, another flannel shirt of a faded red, and a manuscript, which was but a small pile of pieces of paper tied with a string.

Louis Hemon was leaving a lonely backwoods farm, set in a clearing that had grown painfully in size from year to year as the men sweated and strained against trees, alders and stumps. Here he had lived and labored as a hired man for more than a year. Here he had stayed in time of heavy storm and snows, when the tiny log house chinked with mud was like the still center of a hurricane. Here he had toiled in burning the brush, heaving up stumps, swinging his axe against tall spruce and pine. Here he had eaten steaming pea soup and salt pork with this French Canadian family, and watched the women and children work from dawn to dark. He had driven them to Mass in the village, and stood about afterward to talk of what wages were being paid in the lumber shanties, of the early breaking of the ice in the river, and of the terrible droughts one year, or disastrous rains another. He had filled his eyes with the glory of maple leaf in autumn, and with the tender pink haze of new leaf in spring. And all of these things the young man, Louis Hémon, had written into a novel.

Hémon wrote *Maria Chapdelaine*, the story of a French-Canadian girl who must choose between three suitors—her promised husband, who was lost in the snows while trying to visit her after she had chosen him— and then a young man now in good circumstances in the United States

—and a farmer who would give her the same hard life of a pioneer wife that had killed her own dauntless mother while still young. The choice that she made—to remain in the bush with a farmer husband—was that of a hardy French race, a race that still calls itself *Canadien* and all others "newcomers."

In 1913 Louis Hémon was killed in a railway accident not long after leaving Peribonka village, in the "Lake St. John country," which is north of Quebec City. *Maria Chapdelaine* is his one book. Although he was an immigrant from France, his spirit was that of the Canadians who made this land their own in the days of Cartier, Champlain and Frontenac.

Other books have pictured Canada, its different racial groups, and its lands, lakes and forests. Many know the prairie country, and the Scotch communities through the novels of Ralph Connor. Canada has stories of the "blue-nose" Nova Scotians, who are often fishermen, and of the people of Labrador, the sealers as well as the Indians, the voyageurs of Quebec, Ontario and the West—the color of the past and the life of modern Canadians. Early in the last century Thomas Haliburton became known as one of the first humorists in North America, and since then there have been many authors of note such as Mazo de la Roche, novelist; Stephen Leacock, humorist; Bliss Carman and Charles Roberts, poets, with historians and others writing both in French and in English. Toronto is one of the important centers of both French and English language book production in the world.

Music and the theater also flourish in Canada, where there are a number of fine symphony orchestras and choral groups. Festivals of music and drama are big affairs, and the performers of the Stratford Shakespearean Festival have even entertained Eskimos in the far north.

Distinguished Canadian scientists include Sir William Osler and Sir Frederick Banting, who discovered insulin, and for whom the Banting Institute for Medical Research at the University of Toronto is named. Alexander Graham Bell invented his telephone in Canada.

Canada has many painters, sculptors and printmakers, both in the traditional and abstract schools. Their works reflect the long history and the vast variety of Canadian experience. Together with the writers they give us a portrait of Canada—its swift rivers, deep lakes, prairies and high peaks. They show us the Nootka Indians seeking whale on the Pacific coast in boats made of burned-out logs, Eskimos and prospectors of the frozen lands, the Red River Valley, the buffalo, the bear

and the caribou. They give us orchards of the Annapolis Valley, mines in barren lands below Hudson Bay, and Gaspé, old haunt of pirates and ghosts. From writers, artists and musicians we can know the immigrants who settle on farms, and around huge steel mills, and who often continue to speak the languages of Europe. In these works there seems to be the salty sea, the fresh lake winds, the scent of pine, the roar of the mill, and the drone of the bush pilot's plane.

CHAPTER XXXIV   FABULOUS PASSAGE

THE WATERS of the Great Lakes make the world's largest inland seas. From cold Superior in the north they move through rivers to the smaller lakes. With a thundering roar they hurl themselves down the falls of Niagara in a cloud of mist, and twist out of Lake Ontario among a thousand islands into a wide river rushing toward the ocean. This is the mighty St. Lawrence, blue-green and cold, entrance to half a continent. Jacques Cartier called it the River of Canada, although he named the great bay into which it poured the St. Lawrence. With its thousands of lakes and rivers, large and small, Canada has more than half of the fresh water of the world. The St. Lawrence, gateway to this unknown country, is queen of all its rivers.

An English immigrant sailing up the St. Lawrence more than a hundred years ago described the shores: "The white houses, with their high roofs, like those we see in pictures of French chateaux, and the churches roofed with tin, and as white underneath as the others, and the line of fields of every shade, from the brown earth to the dark green wheat, and the curious zigzag wooden fences, and the solemn woods, every here and there coming out at the back of the picture, like great grim sentinels of the land, made it impossible to stay away from the deck."

In summer the river, broadening to a width of ninety miles where it meets the bay, is filled with ocean vessels coming in from world ports, and with small river steamers and cargo craft. Autumn paints the river's shores royally in the scarlet, orange and gold of maple, birch and oak, outlined against dark green of pine and spruce. Birds of forest and water turn southward, soaring away from cold winds.

Then snow falls in great white sheets, covering everything to the tops of fences and the river becomes a road of ice. Canadians enjoy their

cold winters, for it is then that they skim down the mountain slopes on skis, hold winter carnivals, and skate.

Spring is a miracle each year, as pink bud of tree and bush burst into green, and the earth appears brown and ready for the plow. Then the honking of wild geese brings a farmer's head up to watch, and he knows that soon the loon will follow to find its lonely lake, and the noisy raven, the great loud woodpecker and the many quick little singing birds. Soon flocks of scolding gulls will greet the first ships steaming up the river from distant ports, and rafts of logs will surge down the rapids to mills on shore, to be made into pulp for paper.

Down the rivers have flowed the riches of the West, iron, steel, copper, wheat and logs. Yet not until now has man tried to do more than build relatively small locks and canals to bypass waterfalls and rapids, and enable river craft to reach the different levels of the lakes. The huge ocean traffic has been able to go no farther than Montreal. Now beyond that point the St. Lawrence Seaway, a joint project of Canada and the United States, is building a waterway system that will, by 1960, have extended the ocean itself into the heart of the continent. Monster dredges, scoops and bulldozers lift the earth and transform the islands, the shores and the river, with its surging whitewater rapids.

At the International Rapids an enormous power project will give the two countries twelve billion kilowatt-hours of electricity a year. The town of Iroquois has been moved bodily to higher ground to make way for a twenty-seven mile lake in the broadened river. The Seaway, costing many millions of dollars, will make it possible for sea-going freight vessels to steam all of the way to Chicago or to the end of Lake Superior, a distance of 1,500 miles from the Atlantic Ocean. The Welland Canal, entirely in Canada, was built thirty years ago, and is large enough to take the big ships. Seven new locks, twice as long, wide and deep as the twenty-three now in use, will take ocean ships 850 miles beyond their present docks.

When the Congress of the United States authorized the Seaway project, already approved by the Canadian Parliament, towns, cities and villages along the St. Lawrence rang their ancient church bells in celebration. At times in the past Canada has feared, sometimes with good reason, that Americans would try to take the country and make it part of the United States. Now these two strong nations are cementing their friendship in this project, shared between them. Canada, an independent nation, choosing to remain in the British Commonwealth, has taken its place in our time, under its democratic parliamentary government, alongside the other important countries of the world

For many years ore has moved down the lakes from the remote iron ranges of Lake Superior. Now ore will go up the lakes instead, to smelters and steel mills in both countries, from new, rich iron mines in Labrador. Cartier, in his small caravel, was saddened when he realized that the St. Lawrence was not the path to the wealth of the Orient. Today, if he could stand with his brown cloak wrapped about him, and look again at this broad flowing river, he would understand that these waters are indeed the Northwest Passage, not to the treasures of the Far East— but to the living riches of Canada.